This arty page presents the elegance of pre-depression America. European clothing styles were admired, decorations were elaborate, and life was beautiful. Use these artfully designed papers to create your own vision of the past.

1929

by Pam Hammons

MATERIALS: *Design Originals* Legacy Collage Papers (#0526 Two Ladies, #0528 Watches, #0535 Ruth's Letter, #0489 Rust Floral, #0493 Brown Linen, #0496 TeaDye Alphabet) • *Design Originals* Slide Mounts (#0977 White) • *Design Originals* Transparency Sheet (#0557 Family) • *ColorBox* Cat's Eye chalk (Peach, Amber, Burnt Sienna) • Frame • Pop dots • Charm • Adhesive

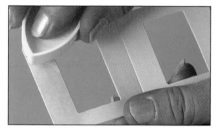

1. Age the edges of slide mounts.

2. Tear numbers.

3. Glue number to Brown paper.

4. Glue numbers inside slide mounts.

INSTRUCTIONS: **Frame cover**: Cut 6" square Watches paper. Glue to frame leaving 3/8" edge all around. Cut corner of paper at an angle to frame 1/8" from corner. Turn paper edges under. Glue to back of frame. • Using craft knife, cut "X" in center of frame opening, corner to corner. Fold paper under to back side of frame. Glue to frame. • Tape photo to back of frame. Tape "Mom" transparency under photo. • **Assemble Page**: Use Ruth's Letter as background paper. Use pop dots to mount frame to page. • .Tear papers as in photo. Use Cat's Eye chalk to antique torn edges.Glue to page. • Tear out "Valisere". Mount on torn Brown Linen. Cut Rust Floral into 1 1/2" squares. Cut Brown Linen into 1 1/4" squares. Tear numbers from TeaDye Alphabet. Layer and glue to page. • Color slide mounts with Cat's Eye chalk. Glue over letters. Glue charm to page.

Covering the Frame with Paper

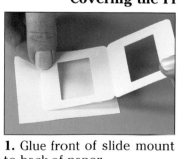

1. Glue front of slide mount to back of paper.

2. Cut center "X".

3. Miter the corners.

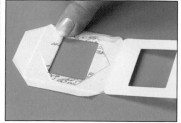

4. Fold the paper to the back and glue.

Kenny & Bernice

by Amy Hubbard

MATERIALS: *Design Originals* Legacy Collage Papers (#0547 Dictionary, #0490 Coffee Linen) • *Design Originals* Slide Mounts (#0978 Black) • *Design Originals* Transparency Sheets (#0556 Word Tags, #0557 Family) • Black cardstock • *Making Memories* Antique Gold shaped circle clips • *Jest Charming* clock hands • Small Gold brads • Pop dots • *JudiKins* Diamond Glaze glue

INSTRUCTIONS: Tear Dictionary paper and mount to cardstock. • Adhere transparency words in slide mounts. Attach circle clips to slide mounts. • Position slide mounts over words "Honor, Love, Faithful" on Dictionary paper. Use pop dots to attach slide mounts to paper. • Crumple Coffee Linen paper for mat and sand to add a distressed finish. Attach mat and photo to layout. • Print caption and title on Coffee Linen paper. Crumple and sand. Glue caption to layout. Use brads to attach title to layout. • Glue clock hands using Diamond Glaze.

1. Swipe Walnut ink across the paper.

2. Trace and cut out the template.

3. Fold and glue envelope.

Wonders of Nature

by Katrina Hogan

MATERIALS: *Design Originals* Legacy Collage (#0553 Map) • *Design Originals* Slide Mount (#0975 Large) • *Autumn Leaves* vellum • Cardstock (Brown, White) • *Making Memories* metal letters • *Stop N Crop* Mesh • *Hero Arts* rubber stamps • Brown polymer clay • *Two Busy Moms* fibers • *Deluxe Cuts* envelope template • Toothpicks • Tacky glue • *Hermafix* adhesive • Eyelets • Small round punch • *Jest Charming* spiral swirl paper clip • *Postmodern Design* Walnut Ink crystals twice diluted • Fine sandpaper • *ColorBox* Roussillon pigment ink • *Memory Makers* game tile stickers

INSTRUCTIONS: Roll clay into a thin sheet. Stamp image into clay. Bake as directed. • Age Brown cardstock with sandpaper. Tear edges. Swipe with Walnut ink. • **Aged Envelopes and tags**: Swipe Walnut ink over White Cardstock. Cut out tags and envelopes. Age edges with pigment ink. • Cut slide mount in half. Apply Walnut ink using a paper towel. • Stain toothpicks with Walnut ink. Cut to size. Glue to slide mount. **Assembly**: Glue Brown cardstock to Map. Tape Vellum in place. Add mesh. Glue photo and embellishments as shown.

1 9 0 4   J o u r n e y

by pj dutton

**Age and stamp slide mounts.
Insert transparency. Tape shut.
Glue to page.**

**Walnut ink gives collage papers an
aged look on this typewriter key tag.**

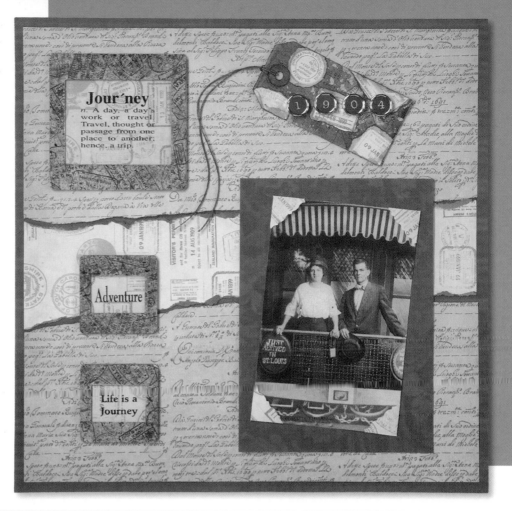

Step back to 1904 with this travel page. The couple in this photo had just arrived in St. Louis. Keep that "turn of the century" feeling by aging slide mounts with ink. The coordinating background papers and tags complete the presentation.

MATERIALS: *Design Originals* Legacy Collage Papers (#0494 Brown Stripe, #0495 Brown Floral, #0548 Passport, #0550 TeaDye Script)• *Design Originals* Slide Mounts (#0975 Large, #0977 White) • *Design Originals* Transparency Sheets (#0561 Travel, #0558 Script) • Crème cardstock • Shipping tag • *Postmodern Design* Walnut Ink crystals (in a spritzer bottle) • Isopropyl alcohol (in a spritzer bottle) • Paintbrush • Rubber Stamps (JudiKins 6803K Travel Bollio; *Stampers Anonymous* SL22484 Typewriter Alphabet and Numbers) • *Ancient Page* ink (Chocolate, Coal) • *Coffee Break Design* 14mm typewriter key frames • *Carl* 1/2" paper punch • *Marvy* photo corner punch • Acetate • PVA Glue • Pencil with eraser • Bone folder • Double-stick tape

INSTRUCTIONS: Trim Passport and Script paper to 11 1/2" x 11 1/2" • Stack Passport and Script paper together. Tear middle section. • Paint torn edges with Walnut ink • Glue Script and Passport paper to Brown Stripe background as shown. • Punch corners for photo from Passport paper. Attach to photo. • Cut photo mat from Brown Floral paper • Mat photo. Glue to page. • Spray slide mounts with walnut ink. Dab ink with paper towel for an aged finish. Let dry. • Stamp mounts with Travel Bollio and Chocolate ink. • Cut transparencies and squares of Passport paper to fit slide mounts. Assemble mounts. • Glue to page.
Shipping Tag: Spray tag and string with Walnut ink. • Spread ink with paintbrush. Spray with Isopropyl alcohol. Let dry. • Stamp tag and string with Chocolate ink and Travel Bollio. • Tear Passport paper. Paint torn edges with Walnut ink. Glue to tag. • Stamp 1-9-0-4 on cardstock in Coal ink using Typewriter Key stamps. Punch out. • Punch 4 circles from acetate and 16 circles from cardstock. • Holding the Typewriter Key frame upside down, stack acetate circle, stamped number, and 4 cardstock circles. Repeat for each frame. • Turn frame over and place it on tag. Apply just enough pressure to mark placement. Remove 3 key frames. • Holding remaining key frame, turn tag over. Using a pencil with eraser, push the eraser on the pointed prongs until prongs poke through tag. • Use bone folder to push prongs down toward the center of frame. • Tape tag to page.

Making the Tag

1. Spray tag and string.

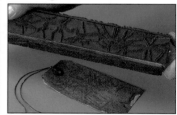

2. Stamp image on tag.

3. Collage tag.

4. Stamp numbers.

5. Punch out numbers.

6. Push prongs with eraser.

1. Trace slide mount onto paper and cut.

2. Glue paper to back.

3. Age edges with ink.

4. Mark and punch holes.

5. Wrap the wire around cylinder.

6. Stack slide mount pages. Twist spiral wire through holes.

Hook slide mounts together with wire spiral to make a book of photos.

Punch hole in slide mount and attach locket with jump ring.

Wedding Page

by Shirley Rufener

MATERIALS: *Design Originals* Legacy Papers (#0490 Coffee Linen, #0479 Green Stripe, #0495 Brown Floral, #0499 TeaDye Music) • *Design Originals* Transparency Sheets (#0558 Script) • *Design Originals* Slide mounts (#0975 Large, #0979 Round) • Cardstock (Mirror Gold, Oatmeal) • Gold embossing powder • Embossing ink pad • StazOn ink pads (Olive Green, Timber Brown, Pumpkin) • *Sizzix* (die cutter, "tags" die #38-0236) • 2 Ivory skeleton leaves • *Xyron* (510 permanent adhesive cartridge, adhesive runner) • *Aleene's* (7800 Adhesive, Memory Glue) • Brown fibers • Brads (1 large and 5 small Gold, 1 small Black) • Hole punch (1/8" and 1/16") • 18" Bronze 22 gauge wire • Antique Gold locket and flower charm with loop • Gold jump ring • Black extra fine tip marker

INSTRUCTIONS: **Pocket:** Ink round slide mount with Olive. • Tear 5" floral strip of paper. Emboss torn edge and slide mount with Gold. • Punch 1/16" hole in top of slide mount. Attach locket to charm with jump ring. Glue charm to bottom of slide mount with 7800. Attach slide mount to pocket with Green brad. Run leaves through Xyron. Add to pocket. Adhere pocket to Coffee Linen page with adhesive runner. Add brads to corners. • **Spiral slide mount:** Cover both sides of 1 large slide mount and 1 side of remaining mount with Green Stripe paper. Glue second layer of Floral paper. Age outer edges with Brown ink. Place photos in slide mounts. Tape closed. • Add spiral hinge (see step-outs). • Mat slide mount spiral with Gold cardstock. Adhere to page with Memory glue. • **Page Assembly:** Double-mat large photo with Green and Gold cardstock. Glue to page. • Die-cut tags from Music, Floral, and Oatmeal cardstock. Trim Oatmeal tag and journal details. • Color tint large brad with Brown and Pumpkin ink. Let dry. Tie tags together with fiber wrapped brad. Place tags in pocket.

The elements here are stitched together the way love holds a couple together. The contrast between soft and hard elements on the page provide balance and meaning. Vellum and leaves are fragile, like a relationship. Metal clock hands remind us to appreciate the time we have together. The words "True Love" are carefully crafted from a computer generated font. Enjoy choosing design elements to express your true love.

1. Tear cardstock.

2. Ink the edges.

3. Wet edges of paper.

4. Roll wet edges.

True Love

by Katrina Hogan

MATERIALS: *Design Originals* Legacy Collage Paper (#0478 Green Linen, #0550 TeaDye Script) • *Design Originals* Slide Mount (#0977 White) • *Design Originals* Transparency Sheets (#0559 Alphabet) • Beige cardstock • *Autumn Leaves* vellum • *DMD* tag • Letter beads • *ColorBox* pigment inks • *Adornaments* fiber • *7 Gypsies* dimensional faux typewriter keys • *EK Success* (sticker typewriter keys, measuring tape) • *Making Memories* "years gone by" eyelet • *Walnut Hollow* clock hands • *All Night Media* Skeleton Leaf • *Creative Imaginations* faux wax seal • *DMC* floss • *Jest Charming* key charm • Mini brad • *Stop N Crop* hinge • French Script MT Font • Cardstock (Olive, Beige) Copper wire • Chalk • Water pen • Pop dots

INSTRUCTIONS: Tear, chalk and roll 3 pieces of Beige cardstock. • Tear hole in center of upper left piece. Back with Script paper. • Poke one end of wire through cardstock and curl. String beads. • Poke other end through cardstock and curl. Glue to background paper. • **Tag section:** Glue vellum and Script paper onto cardstock. • Stamp tag and brush with chalk. Cut off bottom of tag. Hinge tag pieces together. Add embellishments and fibers. Adhere to section with pop dots. • **Photo section**: Apply pigment ink to slide mount. Insert "T". Glue slide mount to page. • Computer print and cut out letters for "rue Love". Glue in place. • Add clock hands with brad. • Layer cardstock, vellum, TeaDye, and photo. • Punch holes on sides of photo for fibers. Add charm and thread fibers through holes to back of page. Tape to secure. • Pierce paper with needle. Add stitching • Add embellishments as shown.

Collage, stamp and chalk tag. Cut off bottom. Hinge pieces together. Add embellishments and fibers.

Ink slide mount. Insert "T". Glue to page. Cut out "rue Love". Glue in place. Add clock hands with brad.

Attach fibers and charm. Glue stickers and seal in place.

Texas
Bluebonnets

by Katrina Hogan

MATERIALS: *Design Originals* Slide Mounts (#0978 Black) • *Design Originals* Transparency Sheets (#0556 Word Tags) • Pop dots • Mini brads • Cardstock

INSTRUCTIONS: Layer cardstock and photos. • Seal transparencies in slide mounts. Attach slide mounts with pop dots. • "Texas" and "Casey" are printed in Green ink on transparency film. "Bluebonnets" and "Spring 2003" are printed in Black ink on the same film. • Transparency is held in place with mini brads.

Attach slide mount with pop dots to give dimension to the page.

Bluebonnets are the very essence of Texas in Spring. While Bluebonnet season is short-lived, you can keep these blooms in season year-round on this freshly picked page.

1. To make oval links, form links on jig.

2. Clip through one side of the ovals.

3. Set eyelets. Connect the slide mounts.

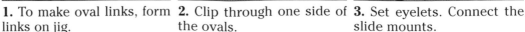

Gold foil and gold ink highlight this "Little Angel". Have fun making a page for your "sugar and spice" girl.

Ribbon hinges make an accordion fold book for your page.

Angel Girl

by Shirley Rufener

MATERIALS: *Design Originals* Legacy paper (#0480 Green Floral, #0493 Brown Linen, #0499 TeaDye Music) • *Design Originals* Slide Mounts (#0977 White, #0975 Large) • *Design Originals* Transparency Sheet (#0557 Family, #0558 Script) • *Design Originals* The Ephemera Book #5207 • *StazOn* ink pads (Olive Green, Pumpkin, Timber Brown, Blazing Red, Mustard) • 5 dauber applicators • Photos • Rubbing alcohol • Large stencil brush • *Gildenglitz* (Variegated metallic leaf flakes, Gold leaf sheet) • Liquid adhesive sizing • $1/2$" flat paintbrush • *Fiskars* deckle edge scissors • $1/8$" eyelets (4 Gold round, 4 Black square) • $1/16$" hole punch • Eyelet punch and setter • Cranberry 22 gauge wire • 6 tiny Gold brads • 8" Mustard Yellow $1/2$" wide ribbon • *Aleene's* (Memory Glue, 7800 Adhesive) • *Xyron* ($1/2$" wide mounting tape, Adhesive Runner) • Antique Brass music note charm

INSTRUCTIONS: Glue 10" square of Green Floral to Brown Linen. • Tear Brown paper and mat photo trimmed with deckle scissors. Glue Music paper to page. Punch corner holes in "Girls" transparency. Set with Gold eyelets. • **Small slide mounts**: Apply sizing to slide mounts. Let dry. Add random Variegated flakes. Fill in remaining White areas with Gold leaf. Burnish with fingertip. • Punch three $1/16$" holes at bottom center of mounts. Add brads. Attach eyelets and wire links. Tape pictures from Ephemera book to back of slide mount. Mat on Brown torn paper. Glue in place. • **Large Accordion Mounts:** Apply ink to large mounts with dauber leaving White areas. Apply second and third color randomly. Immediately stipple with rubbing alcohol. Press and rotate brush in a spiral motion to remove some ink. • Stipple random areas of Green mount with adhesive sizing. Add Gold leaf sparingly. Secure transparency with Adhesive Runner. • Mark and cut one or two slits inside fold of mount with craft knife. • Thread ribbon through slits. • Tape ribbons and image to mount. • Tape ribbon ends inside second mount to hinge. Tape image and mount closed. Use ribbon hinges to link mounts together. Add photos. Glue mount to page. • Accordion-fold remaining large mounts. • Glue music charge with 7800.

Decorate metal-leafed slide mounts with brads. Connect with wire through eyelets.

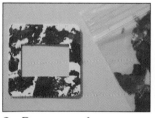

1. Apply a thin layer of adhesive sizing. Let dry.

2. Press random areas with leaf flakes.

3. Apply second leaf color and burnish.

1. Cut slits inside frame mount with craft knife.

2. Push the ribbon through the slits.

3. Tape ribbons and image to slide mount.

4. Attach slide mounts together with ribbon.

Halloween is an opportunity to catch the kids doing some really fun activities. Whether it's pumpkin carving, apple bobbing or dressing up in costume, you will want to scrapbook the excitement. Gather papers in Orange and Brown and set your page aglow with the transparency technique on this page.

1. Insert paper in quilling tool.

2. Roll quilling paper.

3. Remove paper and pinch sides to shape.

4. Glue quilled shapes on paper.

Carving Pumpkins

by Amy Hubbard

Add a decorated transparency to your covered slide mount.

Crumple, tear, and age print words. Add buttons.

MATERIALS: *Design Originals* Legacy Paper (#0487 Rust Linen, #0488 Rust Stripe), *Design Originals* Slide Mount (#0975 Large) • *Design Originals* Transparency Sheet (#0563 Holidays) • Tan cardstock • Vellum • Orange eyelet • *Making Memories* Alphabet Charms • *Rebecca Sower* Typewriter Key alphabet stickers • *Adornaments* Fibers • Buttons • *ColorBox* dye re-inkers (Orange, Green, Yellow) • *JudiKins* Diamond Glaze • *Susie Sparkle* Winter White opaque glitter • White tissue paper • Computer generated font.

INSTRUCTIONS: Prepare transparency following directions given below. Cover slide mount with Rust Stripe. Insert transparency in slide mount and attach to page. • Mount photos on Tan cardstock. Punch holes in top and bottom of matted photos and tie with fibers. Glue to scrapbook page. • Cut jack o lantern photo in tag shape. Write month and year on vellum. Attach vellum to photo tag. Trim vellum. Attach eyelet and fiber to tag. Glue tag to page. • Tear Rust Stripe paper and attach to corners. • Print words on Beige paper. Crumple and tear. Sponge with Rust ink. Glue in place. • Add buttons, stickers, and alphabet charms as shown.

Making the Jack O Lantern Transparency

1. Cover transparency with Diamond Glaze.

2. Add color drops and swirl a little.

3. Sprinkle glitter.

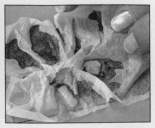

4. Crumple tissue paper and cover the back.

Happy Halloween

by Katrina Hogan

MATERIALS: *Design Originals* Legacy Paper (#0478 Green Linen) • *Design Originals* Slide Mount (#0975 Large) • *Design Originals* Transparency Sheet (#0563 Holidays) • Green cardstock • *Sizzix* die-cutter and leaf die • *Making Memories* Twistel • *Jest Charming* silver swirl paper clip • *Magic Scraps* beads • *Lake City Craft* 1/8" quilling paper (24 Orange strips, 2 Brown strips) • *Plaid* Dimensional Magic • Silk leaves • White gel pen • 3 colors acrylic paint • Sponge

INSTRUCTIONS: **Slide Mount**: Cut slide mount in half. Sponge paint slide mount and back side of transparency. • **Quilling**: Roll 100 Orange 8" marquis shapes. • Roll 10 Brown 6" marquis shapes. • Glue marquis in place, beginning at bottom of pumpkin shape working up and around to fill shape. Add Browns for stem. • **Beaded leaves**: Die-cut 2 leaves. Coat with Dimensional Magic. Cover with beads • **Page Assembly**: Tear cardstock for photo mat. Cut Green mat for slide mount. Glue mats, photo, and slide mount in place. • Glue the embellishments in place.

Abundance

by Katrina Hogan

MATERIALS: *Design Originals* Slide Mount (#0975 Large) • *Sticko* tiles • Cardstock • *Magic Scraps* clearly creative transparency • *JudiKins* crackle stamp • *ColorBox* Gold pigment ink • *Paper Moon* Verdigris embossing powder • *Top Boss* Clear embossing pad • Mini brads

INSTRUCTIONS: Cut Green cardstock mats. Layer mats and photos as shown. • Stamp Gold pigment ink all over surface of slide mount with crackle stamp. • Set ink with heat gun. • Apply clear embossing ink and Verdigris embossing powder. Heat set. • Glue slide mount in position. Add Sticko tiles. Attach "abundance" transparency and pine cone photo with mini brads.

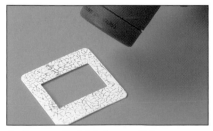

1. Stamp Gold ink on slide mount. Heat set.

2. Stamp clear embossing ink. Add embossing powder. Heat set.

Celebrate the abundance of Autumn with this page embellished using silk leaves and quilling. These colors won't fade, and neither will the memories as you preserve the good times.

Elizabeth Davies

by Jennifer Maughan

Use collage paper inside decorated slide mounts.

MATERIALS: *Design Originals* Legacy Collage Paper (#0487 Rust Linen, #0529 Le Jardin, #0551 Legacy Words) • *Design Originals* Slide Mounts (#0977 White) • Black cardstock • Vellum • Decorative punch • Charms

INSTRUCTIONS: Layer Words paper on Rust Linen paper. • Decorative punch Rust Linen mat for photo. Layer Black and Rust mats with photo. Glue in place. • Write name, city, and date on vellum. Adhere to Rust paper. Glue in place. Add charms. • **Make Side Border:** Cover slide mounts with paper or stickers. Insert cut-outs from Le Jardin paper. Mat on Black cardstock. • Glue Black, Rust, and torn Legacy Words to make base paper. Glue to page. Add matted slide mounts and charms.

Pretty Woman

by Jennifer Maughan

Stretch your supplies and make your pages flatter by cutting slide mounts in half.

MATERIALS: *Design Originals* Legacy Collage Paper (#0526 Two Ladies, #0529 Le Jardin, #0539 Plaid Hanky, #0548 Passport) • *Design Originals* Slide Mounts (#0977 White) • *Bazzill* Black Linen Cardstock • Black glossy cardstock • Charms • Black fine weave *Magic Mesh* • Glue stick

INSTRUCTIONS: Layer Plaid Hanky paper on Black cardstock. • Mat photo with Black Linen, torn Passport paper and Black glossy cardstock. Glue in place. • Mat title with Black Linen and torn Passport paper. Glue in place. • Tear Le Jardin paper. Mat on Black Linen. Glue in place. Add mesh and charms. • Layer small square of mesh, Black Linen, and jewelry charm. Glue in place. • Cut slide mount in half at fold. Cover slide mount with glue stick. Tear bits of Le Jardin paper to cover slide mount. Mat on Black Linen. Add charms. Glue in place.

1. Trace the pattern onto the back of the paper.

2. Make a liner with Cream cardstock.

3. Color the edges of the slide mount with marker.

4. Age the game tiles.

This lovely page is rich with detail and romance of the past. The stamped tissue is reminiscent of 19th century fabrics. These colors could easily be found in any Victorian drawing room. The brown threads and buttons could have graced a gentleman's suit, while the optical lens and chain were surely attached to his vest. All these elements combine in an elegant representation of days gone by.

Pocket Pattern
Fold along dashed rules.
Fold in order given.
Glue in shaded area.

Decorative pockets and classy name plates show off your slide mounts.

Days Gone By

by Mary Kaye Seckler

MATERIALS: *Design Originals* Legacy Paper (#0487 Rust Linen, #0488 Rust Stripe, #0489 Rust Floral) • *Design Originals* Slide Mounts (#0978 Black) • Cardstock (Rust, Cream, Brown) • Kraft tissue • 10 mixed Brown buttons • Brown *DMC* floss • *ColorBox* Chestnut Cat's Eye ink • *Adirondack* Espresso ink pad • *Encore* Gold ink pad • *JudiKins* Gold embossing powder • *F & W* Artist's Acrylic Burnt Umber • Lock and key charms • 2 Brown 1/4" eyelets • Gold mini brads • Antique optical lens with chain • Small game tiles • Rubber stamps (*The Moon Rose* Button border; *Wordsworth* "The Years Tell Us", Memory; *Hero Arts* Old French Writing; *Stampers Anonymous* Tag Block, Baroque Scrap; *Treasure Cay* Locks; *JudiKins* Renaissance Art Stamps) • *Gem-Tac* glue • Black marker • Photos copied onto acetate

INSTRUCTIONS: Stamp Button Border in Espresso ink along bottom and sides of Rust Linen paper. Tie floss in buttonholes. Glue buttons along border. • Stamp Baroque scrap in Espresso ink on Kraft tissue. Tear two pieces. Rub Chestnut ink on edges and glue to corners. • Make envelopes as shown. Smudge edges with Chestnut ink to age. • Assemble slide mount with acetate photo. • Stamp tags on Rust cardstock. Cut out and edge with Chestnut ink. Write names. Glue in place. Attach brads. • Set 2 Brown eyelets to secure optical lens. Position pocket for lens. • Age game tiles with Burnt Umber paint by dabbing with paper towel. Glue tiles to Brown cardstock with Gem-Tac glue. • Emboss 2 word stamps in Gold on Brown cardstock. Mat one on Rust Floral, one on Rust Stripe. • Stamp keyholes in Espresso ink. Adhere key charms and keyhole using Gem-Tac and Gold brads.

Family

by pj dutton

MATERIALS: *Design Originals* Legacy Collage Paper (#0478 Green Linen, #0530 Mom's Sewing Box, #0555 Tags, #0533 Dress Pattern, #0535 Ruth's Letter) • *Design Originals* Slide Mount (#0977 White) • *Design Originals* Transparency Sheets (#0556 Word Tags) • *JudiKins* (Tea Vellum, Diamond Glaze glue) • 3 Shipping tags • Buttons • Floss (Green, Pale Pink) • Sewing needle • Copies of family photos • Rubber Stamps (*Rubber Moon* memories, family, best times, treasured, magic, precious; *JudiKins* 1705G Baby's Arrival) • *Clearsnap* (Ancient Page Sage ink, Bisque Fluid Chalk pad) • *Tsukineko* (*Brilliance* Pearlescent Crimson, *StazOn* Black) INSTRUCTIONS: Center 11" square of vellum to Mom's Sewing Box background. • **Make pockets**: Cut Tags paper 6" x 12". Fold in half to make 3" x 12". Sew to bottom of page (sewing machine or by hand). • Cut Dress Pattern paper 5 1/2" x 4 1/2" mat for photos. Stamp words on vellum using Pearlescent Crimson ink. Mat photos. Glue in place. • **Making Tags:** Sponge Bisque fluid chalk on tag. Let dry. Stamp baby announcement lines in Black ink on bottom half of tag. Write information on tag. Cut pictures and mat with Green linen paper. Glue to tag. Write age in top right-hand corner. Stamp word on the upper left-hand corner. Glue button over tag hole using Diamond Glaze. When glue is dry, thread pink floss through button. • **Make Slide Mount**: Apply Sage ink to surface of slide mount. Wipe with soft towel to blend and remove excess ink. • Stamp words on front of Slide mount using Pearlescent Crimson ink. • Cut square of Ruth's Letter paper. Cut 'Family' square from transparency sheet. Assemble slide mount. • Sew Green floss on button and glue on lower left corner using Diamond Glaze. Glue slide mount in place. • Sew buttons as shown. Place a small dab of Diamond Glaze or tape on back of page to secure thread knots.

The tags in these pockets carry the data as well as the photo of each child. This is a fun and simple project.

Thread buttons and glue to corners. Place tag in pocket.

Cover slide mount with paper, stamps, and embellishments.

1. Fold tag paper in half lengthwise. **2.** Sew to form pockets.

Nursery Rhymes

by pj dutton

MATERIALS: *Design Originals* Legacy Paper (#0497 TeaDye Letters, #0478 Green Linen) • *Design Originals* Heritage Paper (#0409 Nursery Rhymes) • *Design Originals* Slide Mounts (#0979 Round) • *Design Originals* Transparency Sheet (#0559 Alphabet) • *Coffee Break Design* brads • Rubber Stamps (*Stampers Anonymous* Vision Alphabet) • *JudiKins* Color Duster • *Clearsnap* (*Fluid Chalk* Pads - Lime Green, French Blue, Pastel Peach; *Ancient Page* – Pine Green, Indigo, Henna) • Double-stick tape • Photo copied on Canvas Photo Paper • Foam tape

INSTRUCTIONS: Mat 2 strips of Nursery Rhyme paper 2 3/8" x 11" on 2 strips of Green Linen paper. Glue to top and bottom of TeaDye Letters page • Mat photo with Green Linen. Attach to center of page with brads. • Mask window of slide mount. Apply Fluid Chalk ink using Color Duster. Color 2 mounts Green, 2 Blue and 2 Peach. • Stamp letters and numbers in corners of mounts using Ancient page. • Cut out Nursery Rhyme image and transparency element. • Tape transparency and picture to inside of slide mount with double-stick tape. Close mount. • Color edges of slide mount with ink pad. Double-stick tape 2 slide mounts to each side of page. Use foam tape for center slide mounts

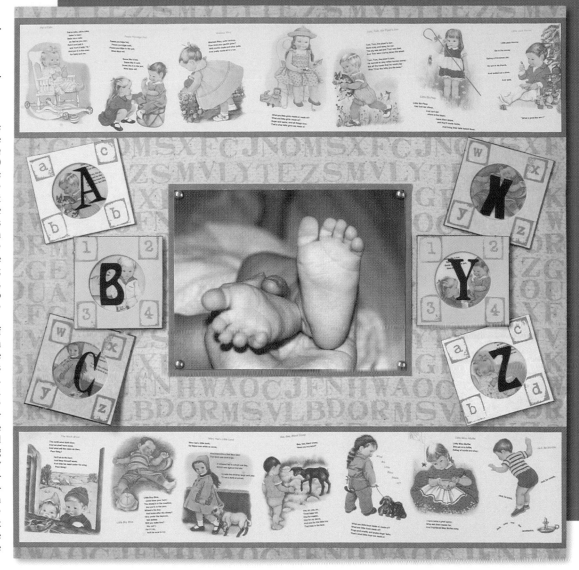

When you make this heartwarming page of your child, don't forget to make one for Grandma too! The Nursery Rhymes decorative paper is perfect for this theme.

1. Mark circle on sticky note with pencil to use as mask.

2. Color the slide mount.

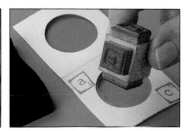

3. Stamp the letters in the corner of the slide mount.

4. Place the slide mount over the image.

5. Sandwich transparency and image in slide mount.

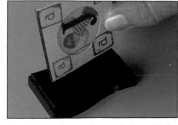

6. Color the edge of the slide mount with ink.

Color slide mount. Stamp letters. Place mount over image. Sandwich transparency and image in mount.

Sew running stitch around Red Patterns paper.

**Tie string in button. Glue button in place.
Glue fabric scraps to page.**

This page takes you back to elementary school with old homework papers, hand-stitched borders, and tied buttons. If your Mom doesn't have some of your old homework papers, check out The Ephemera Book.

Little Angels

by Cindy Pestka

MATERIALS: *Design Originals* Legacy Collage Paper (#0532 Red Patterns, #0535 Ruth's Letter) • *Design Originals* The Ephemera Book (#5207, p. 40) • Red thread • Red buttons • Photo • Fabric scraps • *ArtChix Studio* (Gold stars, wings)

INSTRUCTIONS: Sew running stitch on Red Patterns paper. Glue to Ruth's Letter base. • Glue page from Ephemera book in place. Tie string into buttons. Glue buttons, fabric scraps, photo, angel wings, and stars in place.

This memory of the Family picnic even remembers the ants. The slide mounts create the impression of a red checkered tablecloth in this layout. Take your camera along for the next family gathering so you can make this page for your album.

1. Paint slide mounts Red.

2. Stamp images on mounts.

3. Edge flower with marker.

Family Picnic

by Mary Kaye Seckler

MATERIALS: *Design Originals* Legacy Collage Paper (#0532 Red Patterns), *Design Originals* Slide Mounts (#0975 Large, #0977 White) • *Design Originals* Transparency Sheet (#0559 Alphabet, #0558 Script) • Cardstock (Pink, Black, Tan) • *Jolee's Stickers* (3-D ladybugs, ladybugs, ants) • *Carolee's Creations* picnic basket die-cut • Rubber Stamps (*Penny Black* Scroll Tapestry; *JudiKins* flower cube) • *VersaMark* ink pad • *VersaColor* Cardinal ink pad • Clear embossing powder • *Inkadinkado* chalks • Red Line tape • *Glue Dots International* mini glue dots • *3M* double-stick mounting tape • *Zig* Rose scroll marker • *Aleene's* premium coat Holiday Red acrylic paint • Foam paint brush

INSTRUCTIONS: Paint half the slide mounts with Red acrylic paint. Allow to dry. • Scroll stamp both Red and White slide mounts with Versamark ink. • Tape transparencies into slide mounts. • Affix title to page with glue dots. • Chalk details on basket die-cut. Tape basket to page. • Add ant parade stickers. Draw dots between to indicate motion. • Emboss flower with clear powder on Pink cardstock with Cardinal ink. Trim to size and edge with Rose scroll marker. Edge journaling with Rose pen. Mount on Black cardstock. Add ladybug stickers, gingham flowers and 3D ladybugs. Bend the wings up for added dimension.

Color and decorate slide mounts with transparency letters to make the title in colors to match your picnic table cover.

Cover slide mounts with sticker paper. Vintage ribbon and antique brass brads carry the theme.

Get creative in your embellishment choices. This old key creates nostalgia.

S e w   M u c h   I n   L o v e

by Katrina Hogan

MATERIALS: *Design Originals* Legacy Collage Paper (#0493 Brown Linen, #0549 Shorthand) • *Design Originals* Slide Mount (#0977 White) • *Design Originals* Transparency Sheet (#0559 Alphabet) • French Script MT font • *Nostalgique* Ruler stickers • Brads • *Offray* craft ribbon • Craft knife
INSTRUCTIONS: Cut a 4" x 6" and 8" x 6" piece of Shorthand paper. • Glue to Linen paper as shown. Place sticker as shown. • Cut slide mount in half. Cover slide mounts with stickers and trim excess with craft knife. • Tape transparency letters to slide mount. • Thread ribbon through slide mount. Attach to page with brad. • Print words "much in love". Cut out the words with a craft knife. Glue the words to page.

Carefully cut out computer printed fonts to convey a message in any style you want for your page.

Keys to Happiness

by pj dutton

MATERIALS: *Design Originals* Legacy Paper (#0491 Coffee Stripe, #0492 Coffee Floral, #0493 Brown Linen, #0495 Brown Floral, #0500 TeaDye Keys) • *Design Originals* Slide Mounts (#0975 Large) • *Design Originals* Transparency Sheet (#0560 Objects) • 4 transparent photo corners • Photos • *PVA* glue • Glue brush • Needle tool • 12" Copper 20 gauge wire • Wire cutters • Double-sided tape • Craft knife • 3 old keys • 6 eyelets • Eyelet tools • 30" vintage ribbon

INSTRUCTIONS: **Background Assembly:** Glue 11¹/₂" x 11¹/₂" Coffee Floral paper to Brown Linen base. • Glue ¹/₂" strip of Coffee Stripe 1" from top of page. • Stack and glue 2" Brown Floral, 1" Coffee Stripe, ¹/₂" Coffee Floral, ³/₈" TeaDye Keys as in photo. • **Transparency Mat:** Stack and glue 3³/₄" x 3¹/₄" TeaDye Keys, 3¹/₂" x 3¹/₈" Brown Floral, 3¹/₄" x 2³/₄" Coffee Stripe, 2³/₄" x 2¹/₄" TeaDye Keys. • Cut Transparency 2¹/₄" x 2³/₄". Attach to TeaDye Keys paper with transparent photo corners. Place eyelets and add ribbon. • **Paper covered Slide Mount:** Cut TeaDye Keys 4" x 4". • Glue to the slide mount. • Let dry. Turn over. Cut out window. • Tape photo inside. • Close mount. • Wrap and glue edges of paper to the back of the slide mount. • Place key on the slide mount and mark for wire • Poke holes. • Thread wire around the key to the back of the slide mount. • Position slide mounts and tape to the page. • Center eyelet over slide mount on Coffee Stripe at the top of the page. Thread the ribbon around the key, through the eyelet to the back of the page. Tape to secure.

Ribbon choice, eyelet color, and rustic embellishments add to the nostalgic feel of these heritage pages.
Make a fun and whimsical tag to accent your scrapbook page.

Life Is a Journey Tag

by Shari Carroll

MATERIALS: *Design Originals* Slide Mount (#0978 Black) • *Design Originals* Transparency Sheet (#0561 Travel) • *Nostalgique* typewriter stickers • *Hero Arts* #LL891 letter rubber stamps • *AccuCut* hole reinforcement • *Tsukineko* Brilliance ink • *Memories* dye ink • *Uchida* circle punch • *7 Gypsies* heart clip • Cardboard scrap • Rubber band

INSTRUCTIONS: Cut cardboard. Tear outer paper to expose corrugation. • Stamp various postal type designs onto Black slide-mount using Brilliance ink. • Insert transparency into slide-mount. Glue to cardboard. • Wrap tag with rubber band. Hang clip from rubber band. • Stamp letters on scrap paper. Punch and affix to cardboard. • Attach hole reinforcement tag. Punch hole. Tie fibers to tag.

1. Glue paper to front of slide mount. Let dry.

2. Cut out window.

3. Attach the photo to slide mount.

4. Wrap and glue paper to back of slide mount.

5. Poke holes for wire with needle tool.

6. Thread wire around key to back of slide.

Sisters

by Katrina Hogan

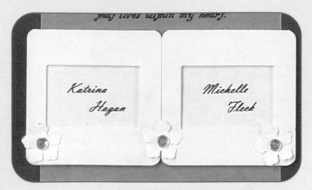

Frame your script in an open slide decorated with punched snowflakes and beads.

MATERIALS: *Design Originals* Slide Mount (#0977 White) • White *Artistic Wire* • Cardstock (Navy Blue, White) • *Making Memories* (eyelet letters, eyelets) • *EK Success* snowflake punch • *Family Treasures* flower stem & leaf punch • 3/8" *Lake City* craft quilling paper • Vellum • Rhinestones
INSTRUCTIONS: Print poem on vellum. Attach to page. • Punch out 9 snowflakes for beaded flower tops. Punch out 3 stems. Glue to page. Add rhinestones. • Mat and mount photos. Add eyelets. • Open slide mount. Print names on White cardstock. Tape names to slide. Glue slide in place. Add snowflake flowers with beads. • **Fringed Flower:** Cut small slits 1/16" apart. Then roll on quilling tool. Glue loose end and remove from tool. • Cut out leaves. Glue wire, leaves and flowers in place.

*Memories of moments
that were made for us to share,
The crazy laughter that's somehow
always there.
Time changes many things
and some dreams come apart,
But nothing can reach or change the love
for you that lives within my heart.*

Making the Fringed Flower

1. Cut small slits 1/16" apart to fringe paper.

2. Glue 1/8" paper to the end of the fringed piece.

3. Roll 1/8" paper until it reaches the fringed piece and continue rolling into a tight circle on quilling tool. Glue the loose end and remove from tool. Use your fingers to open the flower.

Time • Love Tenderness

by Carol Wingert

MATERIALS: *Design Originals* Legacy Papers (#0486 Blue Floral, #0490 Coffee Linen, #0492 Coffee Floral) • *Design Originals* Slide Mounts (#0977 White) • *Making Memories* (clear letter pebbles, eyelets) • *Designs by Pamela* Silver charms • *Jacquard* Lumiere paint • *Adornaments* fibers

INSTRUCTIONS: On Coffee Floral base, layer and glue torn Blue Floral paper. • Paint slide mounts with Silver metallic paint. Let dry. • Computer generate stencil type letters and insert into mounts. • Glue name strip to Blue Floral. Attach photos, computer generated text strip, and letter pebbles. • Sew journal boxes with brown thread. Add metal accents with eyelets. • Tear and glue a strip of Coffee Linen. • Add eyelets. Lace fibers through holes.

As adults, your children will cherish the pages of times like these. Have fun making the memories last, and passing them down later.

Mount computer generated letters. Glue slide mounts in place.

Lacing with Fiber

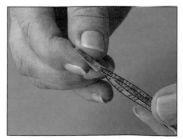

1. Tape end of fiber to form a "needle".

2. Lace fibers through eyelets. Cut off "needle".

3. Tie fibers into a bow.

Decorate slide mounts with jewels and sanded cardstock.

Metal vellum rings make great labels for journaling.

Slide mounts easily transform into shaker boxes. Check out this technique.

Less is more. This charm gives a tranquil touch to this simple slide mount.

Z o d i a c

by Katrina Hogan

MATERIALS: *Design Originals* Slide Mount (#0975 Large) • Cardstock (Blue, Green) • *Carolee's Creations Ting a Lings* Zodiac punchouts • *Making Memories* vellum tags • Metal ring circle tags • Silver brads • Green crystals • Fine grit sandpaper

INSTRUCTIONS: Lightly sand Blue and Green cardstock. • Cover slide mount with Green paper. Glue elements in place as shown.

Pastel colors, vellum, and crystals produce a soft, feminine look on this page.

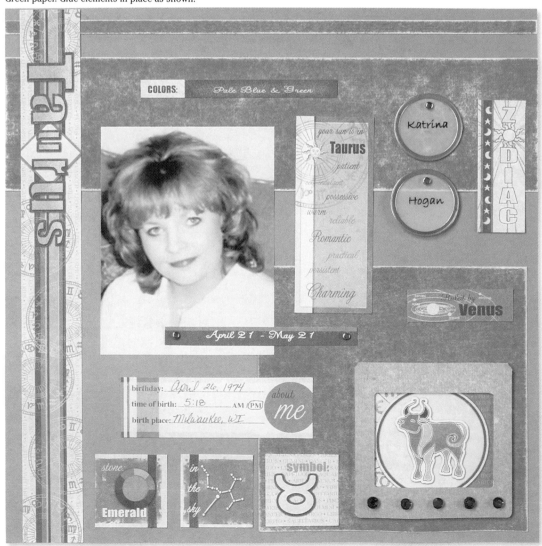

Punchouts add extra zest to your scrapbook pages.

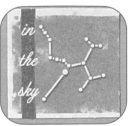

1. Tape the transparency in a slide mount.

2. Foam tape the inside edges of slide mount.

3. Fill with micro beads.

4. Tape the acetate to the back of slide mount.

5. Remove foam tape backing. Join slide mounts.

The silver beads in the shaker box shift like sand on this page. The blue background paper is a great choice to convey a sense of water.

My Dad

by Katrina Hogan

MATERIALS: *Design Originals* Slide Mount (#0975 Large, #0977 White) • *Design Originals* Transparency Sheet (#0557 Family) • Light Blue textured cardstock • *Nunn Design* dragonfly charms • *Making Memories* word eyelets • *Halcraft* micro beads • Fine grit sandpaper • Double-sided foam tape

INSTRUCTIONS: Sand Blue cardstock. This texture effect only works with cardstock that has White core. • Make a shaker box. • Layer 1/2" strips. Glue photo mats in place. Add word eyelets. • Position Blue vertical stripe. Glue small slide mounts in place. Add dragonfly charms. • **Shaker Box using Slide mounts:** Cut a large slide mount in half at seam. • Tape transparency to inside of top slide mount. Line rectangle opening with double-sided foam tape. (Do not remove tape backing or beads will stick to it) • Place beads inside rectangle. Seal hole in back slide mount with clear transparency or background paper. Peel backing from foam tape and place the back of the slide mount on the front. Glue to layout.

Paper Techniques

1. Tear cardstock to test for White core.

2. Sand for texture.

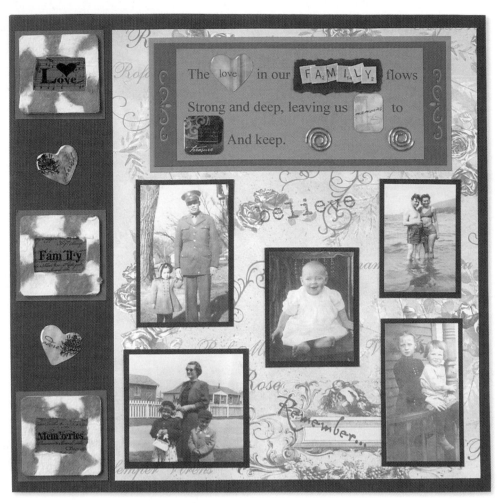

Nostalgic elements make this heritage page interesting. Romantic paper, hole punches, and stamps work well with the slide mount border bearing "Love", "Family", and the "Memories" this page preserves.

Love in Our Family

by Jennifer Maughan

MATERIALS: *Design Originals* Heritage Paper (#0414 Roses and Letters) • *Design Originals* Slide Mount (#0977 White) • *Design Originals* Transparency Sheet (#0558 Script) • *Bazzill* cardstock (Lavender, Purple Light Green, Dark Green, Brown) • Mulberry paper • *Creative Imaginations* Poemstones • *Emaginations* border punch • *Making Memories* spiral clips • Rubber stamps (*Stamp Rosa* "Remember"; *Impression Obsession* "believe") • Game tile stickers • Glue stick

INSTRUCTIONS: Glue 9¼" x 11¼" Heritage paper to page. • Mount photos on Brown cardstock. Glue to page. • Stamp "Remember" and "believe" on page. Print words to make journal box. • Punch Dark Green mat. Layer and glue journal box to page. Add embellishments.• Glue stick surface of slide mount. Cover with torn bits of Purple and Yellow Mulberry paper. • Layer 2 transparencies in slide mount. Mat on Lavender cardstock. Glue in place. Add poemstones.

Collage mulberry paper for added texture.

Dried flowers give your page a natural feeling.

Wedding Day

by Katrina Hogan

MATERIALS: *Design Originals* Heritage Paper (#0244 Tiny Pink Roses) • *Design Originals* Slide Mount (#0975 Large) • *Design Originals* Transparency Sheets (#0558 Script) • Rose cardstock • *YLI* (ribbon, ribbon roses) • 13 Pink Eyelets • *Fiskars* wavy edge scissors • Fine grit sandpaper • Rose charm

INSTRUCTIONS: **Top Section:** Sand Rose cardstock. Trim ends with wavy edge scissors. Mat and glue large photo in place. Set 10 pink eyelets around large photo. Thread and twist ribbon through eyelets. Glue silk flower in place. • **Bottom Section:** Cut slide mounts in half at fold. Cover slide mounts with Pink Roses paper. Wrap ribbon around slide mount. Tape photos and transparency to slide mount. • Sand, trim, and glue Rose cardstock in place • Attach ribbons to page with eyelets. Glue transparent ribbon and silk flowers in place. • Add rose charm to transparency.

First Communion

by Amy Hubbard

MATERIALS: *Design Originals* Slide Mounts (#0977 White) • *Design Originals* Transparency Sheet (#0556 Word Tags) • Cardstock (Purple, Lavender) • Vellum • Purple eyelets • *Hero Arts* Italian Poetry stamp • *ColorBox* ink • *Dress it up* buttons • *Darice* dried flowers • *Offray* White organza ribbon

INSTRUCTIONS: Layer cardstock. • Print title and attach to page. • Stamp slide mounts with script background. Sponge ink around edges. • Insert transparency and flowers in slide mounts. Attach to page. • Attach vellum with eyelets. Attach photo. • Glue ribbon bow and buttons to layout.

Ribbons and roses carry the romance of one of the most celebrated days in a life.

Make ribbon hangers for your decorated slide mounts.

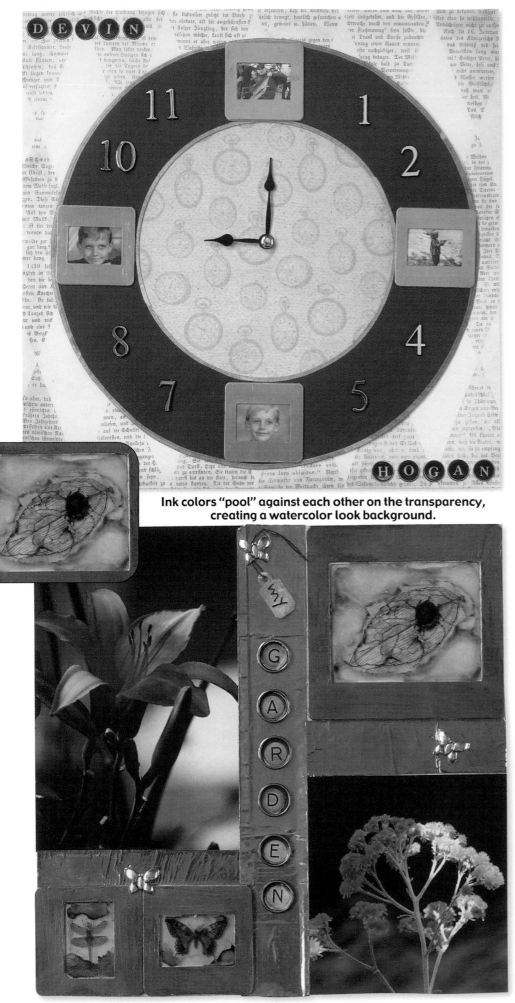

Ink colors "pool" against each other on the transparency, creating a watercolor look background.

Making time for family is very important. This page sends a special message of love to a child.

Show your child how much he is valued when you emboss his photo in Gold.

Time for Devin

by Katrina Hogan

MATERIALS: *Design Originals* Legacy Collage Paper (#0501 TeaDye Clocks, #0554 Diamonds) • *Design Originals* Slide mount (#0977 White) • Chocolate Brown cardstock • *Jest Charming* (Clock hands, numerals) • *Krylon* gold leafing pen • Gold embossing powder • 7 *Gypsies* dimensional faux typewriter keys
INSTRUCTIONS: Emboss slide mounts. Insert photos. • Cut an 11" circle of Chocolate Brown for clock face. • Find center of clock face and cut a 6" circle inside the 11" circle. Gold leaf both edges of Brown circle. • Glue TeaDye Clocks paper to fill the center hole. Glue clock to Diamonds paper. Attach slide mounts, clock hands and clock numerals. Add typewriter stickers.

Joy and serenity accompany this page full of garden pleasures.

My Garden

by Carol Wingert

MATERIALS: *Design Originals* Slide Mounts (#0975 Large, #0977 White) • *Design Originals* Transparency Sheet (#0562 Nature) • Tan cardstock • *Jacquard* Lumiere paint (Copper, Bronze) • *Studio 2* alcohol inks • *Nunn Design* metal letter holders • *Woo Hoo Wowies* butterfly charms • *Rebecca Sower Designs* letters • *Memory Lane* jewelry tag • *Anima Designs* Copper tape
INSTRUCTIONS: Paint slide mounts (2 small, 1 large) with Copper and Bronze. Let dry. • Paint transparency back with alcohol ink. Apply inks (lightest color to darkest) directly from bottle. Inks will "pool" against each other, creating watercolor look. Let dry. Insert transparencies into slide mounts. • Cover cardstock with Copper tape. Glue photos, slide mounts, letters, tag and charms in place.

Alcohol inks create amazing effects on transparencies.

Trick or Treat

by Pam Hammons

MATERIALS: *Design Originals* Legacy Paper (#0487 Rust Linen) • *Design Originals* Paper (#0209 Orange Cobwebs) • *Design Originals* Slide mount (#0978 Black) • *Design Originals* Transparency Sheets (#0563 Holidays) • Cardstock (Black, Orange) • *Hero Arts* Halloween stamps • Black ink pad • Blue Opal *Golden Glaze* • *Sakura* Silver marker • *Fiskars* wavy edge scissors

INSTRUCTIONS: Cut 3 Cobweb papers to fit Black slide mounts. Stamp small spider onto center of 1 rectangle. • Drip Golden Glaze onto top of 3 Black slide mounts. Let dry. • Glue 2 Halloween transparencies to small Cobweb rectangles. Glue inside the slide mounts. Cut Orange cardstock with wavy scissors and mat slide mounts. • Tear Cobweb paper. Glue to the Black cardstock. Stamp spiders and bats on Cobweb paper. • Tear Rust Linen. Glue to page. Glue slide mounts to Rust Linen strip. Draw cobweb onto edge of Black cardstock. Mat photos on Black cardstock. Glue to page.

Spider Web Pattern

Boo!

by Susan Keuter

MATERIALS: *Design Originals* Legacy Paper (#0487 Rust Linen, #0490 Coffee Linen) • *Design Originals* Slide mount (#0978 Black) • *Bazzill* Black cardstock • Font (FleaMarket by Sharon Soneff) • Muslin • Brads • *Suze Weinberg* Ultra Thick Embossing Enamel • Embossing pad • Ink jet printer • Freezer paper • Heat gun

INSTRUCTIONS: Press freezer paper to the back side of muslin with warm iron. Trim fabric to match the paper. Run a piece of tape across the top of the fabric so fabric will feed smoothly through the printer. Load paper into printer to create journaling. Allow ink to dry before removing freezer paper. • Mat Black and Coffee Linen cardstock with photo. Glue to page. • Attach muslin to page with brads. Pull threads to fringe. • Swipe slide mount with embossing pad. Cover Black slide mounts with UTEE. Heat to a bumpy texture. Let cool. • Insert picture. Close the slide mount. Glue to the page.

> Slide mounts can be SCARY! Frost them with ghostly ooze, or make them Black and bumpy. These embellishments complement the patterns and colors of the season.

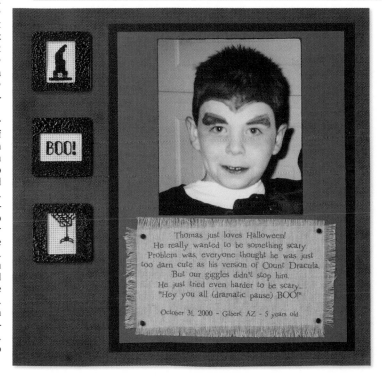

1. Press shiny side of freezer paper to wrong side of fabric.

2. Trim fabric to same size as paper for printer.

Whether it's your first house or your retirement home, your castle deserves a page of its own! Enjoy making this terrific hinged page.

Our Home

by Katrina Hogan

Mat photo and journal box to background paper.

Roof Pattern

MATERIALS: *Design Originals* Legacy Papers (#0480 Green Floral, #0484 Blue Linen, #0486 Blue Floral, #0490 Coffee Linen, #0491 Coffee Stripe, #0494 Brown Stripe, #0497 TeaDye Letters, #0498 TeaDye Tapestry) • *Design Originals* Slide Mounts (#0977 White) • *Design Originals* Transparency Sheets (#0556 Word Tags) • Black cardstock • 4 Black mini brads • *JewelCraft* doorknob • *Stop n Crop* hinges

INSTRUCTIONS: **Base Layer**: On Blue Linen base, mat Black cardstock, torn Blue floral, TeaDye Tapestry, and "Our House" letters. Glue in place. • Mat Blue floral, TeaDye Letters, photo, and journaling to be covered by house. • **Make House**: Using photo as guide, cut out house from Coffee Linen. Cut 2 Coffee Stripe walls 4" x 6³/4". Cut Brown Stripe (door: 1¹/4" x 3", roof: 2¹/4" x 7", 2 roof triangles from pattern). Glue in place. • Tear Green floral for bushes. Glue in place. • Insert transparency in slide mount and cover with Brown Stripe. Glue in place. Add doorknob. • Turn house over and cover back with TeaDye Letter paper. • Hinge house in place.

Give your patriotism an outlet with these spirited papers, stars and transparencies.

Paper choice determines the look of a covered transparency.

American Spirit

by Katrina Hogan

MATERIALS: *Design Originals* Legacy Paper (#0484 Blue Linen) • *Design Originals* Heritage Paper (#0438 Stars & Stripes on Ivory) • *Design Originals* Slide Mount (#0977 White) • *Design Originals* Transparency Sheet (#0556 Word Tags) • Tan cardstock • *ColorBox* Brown fluid chalk • Star brads • Computer generated font

INSTRUCTIONS: Glue 10" x 12" Blue Linen to Tan cardstock. Glue Song in place. Glue Stars & Stripes border. Glue photos. • Insert transparency into slide mount. Cover slide mount with Stars & Stripes paper. Glue in place. • Add star brads. Chalk edges of Tan background.

D a d

by Jennifer Maughan

MATERIALS: *Design Originals* Legacy Collage Paper (#0487 Rust Linen, #0551 Legacy Words) • *Design Originals* Slide Mounts (#0977 White) • *Design Originals* Transparency Sheets (#0557 Family) • Blue cardstock • *Creative Imaginations* Poemstones "moments" • *Magic Scraps* corkboard • *Nostalgique* old ruler sticker • small Black brads INSTRUCTIONS: Cover slide mounts with ruler stickers. Insert photos. Glue in place. • Mat photos with Rust Linen paper. Adhere to page. • Print journaling on vellum. Attach to Rust Linen mat and page with small brads. • Attach "Dad" transparency to cork and page with brads. • Tear Legacy Words. Adhere to vellum. Attach vellum to Rust Linen and page with brads. Add poemstone

Dad pages aren't just for Father's day. Remember all the special events, the special times and don't forget the Dad stories.

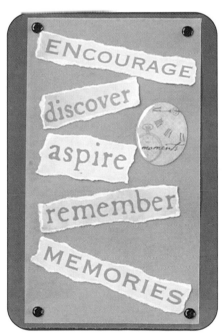

Collage words from papers, or write your own expressions on a vellum tag.

Cork gives a masculine and natural feel when used to mat transparencies.

Stickers are an easy way to collage slide mounts.

Covering Slide Mount

1. Cover slide mount with ruler sticker.

2. Cut out the center of the slide mount.

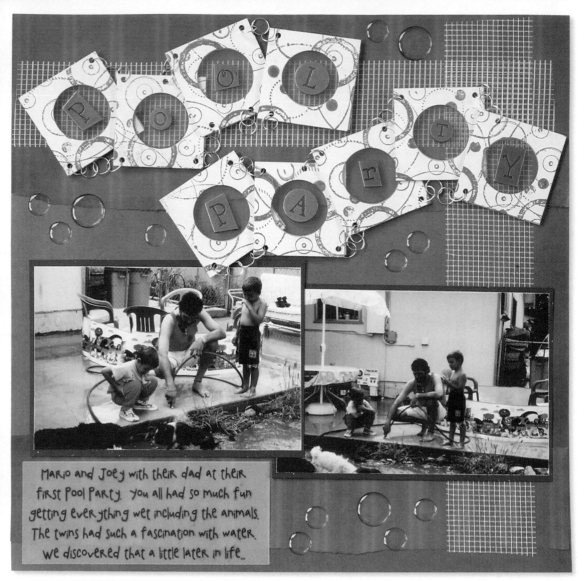

Pool Party

by Tim Holtz

MATERIALS: *Design Originals* Legacy Papers (#0484 Blue Linen, #0485 Blue Stripe) • *Design Originals* Slide Mounts (#0979 Round) • *Ranger* (Archival Cobalt ink pad, Glossy Accents, non-stick Craft Sheet) • *Making Memories* metal letters • *Artistic Wire* (22 gauge Silver wire, wire cutter) • *Crafter's Pick* (Memory Mount, The Ultimate!) • Vellum • *Just for Fun* circles rubber stamp • *Magic Mesh* INSTRUCTIONS: **Making Title:** Mask center of slide mount. Stamp with Archival Cobalt ink. Glue metal letters to inside with The Ultimate!. • Wrap 22 gauge wire around a pencil. Remove and cut coil down the center to make jump rings. • Link slide mounts together. **Page Assembly**: Glue torn Blue Stripes to Blue Linen background. Apply adhesive mesh. • Glue linked slide mounts to page for title. Mat photos and add to page. Print text on vellum and add to page. **Make Bubbles**: Apply Glossy Accents to non-stick craft sheet in various size drops. Let dry completely. Peel off craft sheet and glue with Glossy Accents.

Mario and Joey with their dad at their first pool party. You all had so much fun getting everything wet including the animals. The twins had such a fascination with water, we discovered that a little later in life...

This page is definitely "All Wet". Round slide mounts stamped with circles, metal jump rings, and bubbles make this page fun. Even the mesh reminds you of the rough surface surrounding a pool.

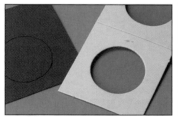

1. Create a mask for the center circle. Stamp image.

2. Glue letter in place.

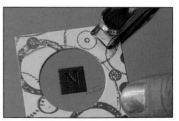

3. Punch holes in the corners of mounts.

4. Cut jump rings apart.

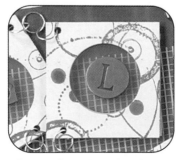

Create dimension by gluing letters on top of the slide mount acetate.

Interlocked jump rings connect slide mounts.

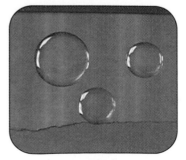

Make your own water bubbles with Glossy Accents. Just drop on non-stick sheet and let dry.

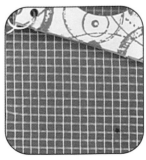

Mesh makes the non-skid pool surround.

Island TV

by Tim Holtz

MATERIALS: *Design Originals* Legacy Collage (#0553 Map) • *Design Originals* Slide Mounts (#0975 Large) • Cardstock (Red, Tan) • *Ranger* (Ink: Archival Maroon, Coffee, Black; Mini brayer) • *Artistic Wire* (22 gauge Silver wire, wire cutter) • *Crafter's Pick* (Memory Mount, The Ultimate!) • *7 Gypsies* metal posts • Mini brads • *Magenta* Flower rubber stamp

INSTRUCTIONS: Brayer slide mounts with Maroon ink. Stamp with Black ink. Use Memory Mount to glue pictures to slide mounts. • Punch holes in slide mounts as in photo. Wrap 22 gauge wire around end of pencil. Remove and cut coil down the center to create jump rings. • Link slide mounts together. • Secure to page on metal posts using The Ultimate!. • Computer print text on cardstock. Distress paper with Archival Coffee ink. Glue to page. Embellish corners with brads. • Mat photo and add to page.

Torn paper backgrounds are a good way to set off your photos.

Metal bar posts act as hangers while jump rings connect the slide mounts.

University of Nebraska - the Columns at Ed Weir Track

When I took this photo of our children, I did not realize these are the same columns on campus where I used to meet their Dad after class. Places can have great meaning and great memories. This page stores the whole story in an envelope.

Old books decorated the first letter of a page. Use this technique to jazz up your titles.

This richly decorated slide mount holds the journaling and is stored inside the envelope.

Memories Pocket Page

by Susan Keuter

MATERIALS: *Design Originals* Legacy Collage Paper (#0552 Travels, #0555 Tags) • *Design Originals* Slide Mount (#0975 Large) • *Design Originals* Transparency Sheet (#0559 Alphabet) • *Bazzill* Linen cardstock (Cream, Green) • Ultra Thick Embossing Enamel • Ink pads • *Waxy Flax* fibers • *Ink It!* charms • Eyelet • Twill tape • Rubber Stamps (*Hero Arts* alphabets, words) • Brown envelope

INSTRUCTIONS: **Page Assembly**: Mat photo with Cream and Green cardstock. Glue in place. • Print journaling on twill tape. Attach to page with brads. •

Envelope: Cut or tear Tags paper to mat behind transparency. Glue transparency and paper to envelope. Stamp remaining letters and words. Add charms, eyelets, safety pin. • **Slide Mount**: Print journaling on cardstock to fit in slide mount. • Color slide mount with Green and Red ink. Glue strips of Travels paper to slide mount. Emboss slide mount with UTEE. • Insert journaling and close slide mount. Punch hole in slide mount corner. Add round paper clip. Tie to envelope string.

Pets are family too. Enjoy embellishing their special page with covered or inked slide mounts, tags, fibers and of course...those purr-fect papers!

Good Pals

by Katrina Hogan

MATERIALS: *Design Originals* ScrapHappy Paper (#0476 Bow Wow Puppy) • *Design Originals* Slide Mounts (#0977 White, #0979 Round) • *Design Originals* Transparency Sheet (#0556 Word Tags) • Cardstock (Cream, Chocolate Brown, Medium Brown) • *Over The Moon press* Brown paw print paper • *EK Success* number stickers • *Making Memories* metal letters • *Stamptacular* metallic rub-ons • *Adornaments* fibers • *ColorBox* Amber Clay fluid chalk • Tags • Shaped buttons
INSTRUCTIONS: Mat photo with 2 layers of cardstock. Glue to page. Add embellishments. • Cover slide mount with Bow Wow Puppy paper. Insert transparency backed with cardstock. Glue slide mount to page. Cover slide mount with paper. Insert photo. Mat with torn Bow Wow Puppy paper and Brown cardstock. Glue cut out numbers. Add fibers. Glue to page. **Tags:** Stipple brush tags with fluid chalk. Tear Bow Wow paper. Chalk edges. Layer and glue to tag with names. Add fibers. • **Title:** Layer light and dark Brown cardstock and torn Bow Wow paper. • Ink slide mounts with fluid chalk. Close slide mounts. Glue metal letters on top. • Glue tags to page.

Cut the tags to carry the film strip theme as you remember your own family actor by creating their very special page.

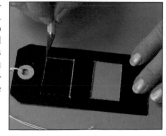

Slide mounts are so versatile. Color or cover them. Insert transparencies or glue letters on top to create texture.

Psalm
by Cindy Pestka

MATERIALS: *Design Originals* Legacy Collage Paper (#0496 TeaDye Alphabet, #0499 TeaDye Music, #0526 Two Ladies) • *Design Originals* Transparency Sheet (#0556 Word Tags, #0560 Objects) • *Artchix* Glamour Girls transparency • Black Cardstock • Tag • Buttons • Ribbon bow • string
INSTRUCTIONS: Cut out name letters. Mount to Black cardstock. • Glue to top of Music paper. Tape Glamour girls transparency to page. Glue photo and ribbon in place. • Cut rectangles out of tag. Tape transparencies to tag. Add string. Glue to page. • Cut label from Two Ladies paper. Glue in place. • String buttons. Glue to the page.

1. Cut windows in tag.

2. Color edge of window with marker.

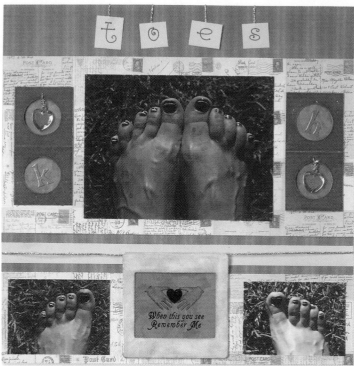

H i p   C h i c k

by Shirley Rufener

MATERIALS: *Design Originals* Legacy Paper (#0491 Coffee Stripe) • *Design Originals* Slide mounts (#0975 Large, #0978 Black, #0979 Round) • Cardstock (Yellow, Lime, Orange) • *StazOn* ink pads (Jet Black, Pumpkin) • *Brilliance* Cosmic Copper ink pad • 3 dauber applicators • *Xyron* (Mounting Tape, Adhesive Runner) • Photos • Vellum • *JewelCraft* multi round mirrors • *Aleene's* Glitter & Gem glue • Flat buttons • Brown suede fringed trim • Mini pony beads • Foam adhesive dots
INSTRUCTIONS: Triple mount Stripe, Lime and Yellow papers on Yellow background with Adhesive Runner. • Color 1 large slide mount solid Black using dauber. Stipple Black mounts with Copper using dauber. • Mask windows of 3 round mounts with cardstock cut to opening shape. Sponge with Pumpkin ink. Use cotton swab with rubbing alcohol to remove mistakes on transparency film. • Cut fringe length slightly smaller than slide mount width. Add beads to fringe with dot of Gem glue. Secure trim to inside of slide mount with mounting tape. Add photos to Black mounts. • Glue buttons and mirrors as shown. • Adhere printed title vellum to Orange cardstock. • Secure Black mounts with foam dots. Secure Pumpkin mounts and title with Mounting Tape.

T o e s

by Katrina Hogan

MATERIALS: *Design Originals* Legacy Paper (#0411 Letter Postcards, #0479 Green Stripe, #0480 Green Floral) • *Design Originals* Slide mount (#0975 Large, #0979 Round) • *Design Originals* Transparency Sheets (#0556 Word Tags) • Lime Green cardstock • *Hallmark* heart charms • *Making Memories* metal letters • *Jest Charming* Gold whimsical wire • *ColorBox* pigment inks • *Suze Weinberg* Ultra Thick Embossing Enamel (UTEE) • *Stamp N Stuff* embossing powder • *Versamark* clear embossing ink • Craft knife
INSTRUCTIONS: **Marble Crackling**: Sponge inks at random. Sponge versamark over entire surface. Cover surface with UTEE. Shake off excess and set with heat gun. Repeat until surface is glassy looking. To further crackle surface, place in freezer for few minutes. Remove from freezer and bend, creating crackle look. • **Small Slide Mounts**: Remove acetate from 2 round slide mounts. Sponge clear versamark ink. Apply Green embossing powder. Shake off excess. Heat set. • Repeat if necessary. • **Assembly**: Layer Green Stripe, Postcards, Lime Green Stripe. • Add photos and embellishments as in photo.

Layer paper behind slide mounts for an accent. Charms add a nice touch to your page.

It's definitely Girl Time! Check out the beaded fringe and hip 60's colors. Maybe it's too nice out to stay indoors. Go sit outside and paint your toenails. Or stay in and make a woven ribbon memory page of those special "girl times".

J u s t   U s   G i r l s

by Susan Keuter

MATERIALS: *Design Originals* Slide Mounts (#0978 Black) • Cardstock • *May Arts Inc.* gingham ribbons • *Diane Ribbons* bead letters • *Creative Imaginations* stickers • *Making Memories* Silver heart eyelet • Eyelets • Brads • Staples
INSTRUCTIONS: Make mat for journal box with 4 squares of cardstock. Glue to page. Add heart charm. • Wrap ribbon around slide mount as in photo. Add photo. Close slide mount. Add knot, eyelet, brad, or staple to decorate ribbon. • Glue slide mounts in place. Weave ribbon and tape to back of page. • Add stickers and beads.

Add a little sparkle and a lot of dimension with star brads.

1. Press prong to mark the hole positions.

2. Punch the holes with the needle tool.

Parents love to document the first day of school. I hope this bright yellow bus makes a stop on your page!

Back to School

by Katrina Hogan

MATERIALS: *Design Originals* Scrap Happy Papers (#0454 Tiny Stars on Red, #0455 Tiny Stars on Blue) • *Design Originals* Slide Mounts (#0978 Black) • Cardstock (Red, Yellow) • *Family Treasures* die cut assortment "School" • *Creative Imaginations* extreme eyelets • *Zig* pen • Star brads
INSTRUCTIONS: Mat photo with Red solid and Tiny Stars on Blue. Glue in place. Add apple die-cuts to photo corners. • Tear Tiny Stars on Blue. Glue to top of page. • Cut out Black letters for title and 3/4" Yellow squares. Glue in place. • Use pattern to cut out Bus. Glue bus to page. Attach wheels with eyelets. • Insert pictures into slide mounts. Glue in place. Add star brads. • Use pencil die-cut for journaling box.

Bus Pattern
You may enlarge or reduce
pattern on a copy machine
to fit your needs.

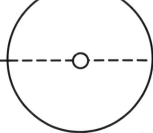

Mario and Joey's first train ride on the Grand Canyon Railroad. What a beautiful day at the Grand Canyon. Your father was so happy taking pictures with you both - nothing but smiles. All aboard.

Subtle colors and rough textured papers mix well with metal embellishments to create a page your men will enjoy.

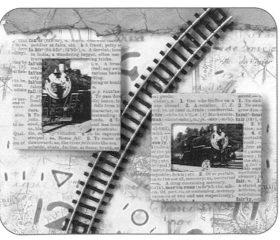

The metal embellishments on this page really fit the theme.

The Train

by Tim Holtz

MATERIALS: *Design Originals* Legacy Collage (#0547 Dictionary) • *Design Originals* Slide Mounts (#0975 Large, #0977 White) • Cardstock (Tan, Brown) • *7 Gypsies* "Magnetique" paper • *Ranger* Archival Sepia ink pad. • *Crafter's Pick* (Memory Mount, The Ultimate!) • *Making Memories* (metal letters, brads) • Train track • Glue stick • Glue dots • Pop dots
INSTRUCTIONS: Cut slide mount in half. Glue slide face down on back of Dictionary paper with glue stick. • Cut paper corners at angle with scissors. • In the center, slice an "x" with craft knife. • Apply glue to slide mount and wrap paper around to back. • Glue photos to slide mounts and page using Memory Mount. Add metal letters to slide mount. • Print text from computer on cardstock. Distress cardstock using Sepia ink. Tear and ink edges. • Mat photo with distressed cardstock. Glue to page. • Add brads to metal letters for title. Attach metal letters with glue dots. Glue track to page with The Ultimate!. • Glue small slide mounts in place with pop dots.

Looking for masculine themes in your scrapbook pages? Check out the bold fonts, background paper, covered slide mounts and clean embellishments. Everything about this page says "photo shoot".

Mario and Joey in their first BIG photo shoot. Following their dreams to be models – and why not? Just look at them..

Here's an interesting way to use those old film negatives!

Finding a transparency that perfectly matches your theme is really fun.

Camera Ready

by Tim Holtz

MATERIALS: *Design Originals* Legacy Collage (#0543 Brushes, #0545 Ledger) • *Design Originals* Slide Mounts (#0975 Large, #0978 Black) • *Design Originals* Transparency Sheets (#0560 Objects) • Vellum • Brown cardstock • *Making Memories* (metal text, brads) • *Crafter's Pick* (Memory Mount, The Ultimate!) • 40 gauge Copper sheet • Film negatives • Pop dots
INSTRUCTIONS: **Cover Slide mounts**: Cut 2 large slide mounts in half. Glue slide face down on back of paper with glue stick. • Cut paper corners at angle with scissors. • In the center, slice an "x" with craft knife. • Apply glue to slide frame and wrap paper around to back. • Wrap one slide mount with Copper paper. • **Assemble page**: Attach old film negative strip to page using The Ultimate!. Glue photos to slide frames and page using Memory Mount. • Insert camera from Object transparency into small Black slide mount. Attach to page with pop dots. • Computer print text on vellum and secure to page with brads. • Mat photo and glue to page. • Glue metal text eyelet to Copper slide frame with The Ultimate!.

Turn a slide mount into a stamped shaker box.

Slide mounts become shaker boxes to display memorabilia conveniently on a page. Decorate your slide mount surface to match the contents and carry the theme.

Key to Friends

by Tim Holtz

MATERIALS: *Design Originals* Legacy Collage Papers (#0542 Father's Farm, #0551 Legacy Words, #0490 Coffee Linen, #0500 TeaDye Keys) • *Design Originals* Slide Mounts (#0975 Large, #0978 Black) • *Design Originals* Transparency Sheets (#0560 Objects) • *Ranger* (mini brayer, Archival Coffee & Black ink pad) • *Crafter's Pick* Memory Mount • *American Tag* shipping tags • *Stampers Anonymous* rubber stamps • Black foam board • Craft knife • Metal ruler • Cutting mat • Rusty keys • Mini brads • Clear acetate • Jute • Glue dots • *Magic Mesh*

INSTRUCTIONS: For large shaker slides, brayer surface of slide mount with Coffee ink and stamp key image with Black ink. • Cut slide mount in half and place on Black foam board. Trace outline of slide with stylus tool. Cut using a craft knife and metal ruler (inside & out). • Glue foam frame to Keys paper using Memory Mount. Fill shaker slide with rusty keys. • Cut acetate to fit frame and glue to top. • Glue slide mount to frame. • Glue shakers to page.

PAGE ASSEMBLY: On Father's Farm base paper, glue torn strip of Words paper and mesh as in photo. • Glue shaker to page. • Glue photo matted with Coffee Linen paper in place. • Computer print text on craft paper. Distress printed paper and tags using Coffee ink. Attach printed paper with brads. • Stamp title on tags using Black ink and alphabet rubber stamps. Add jute fibers. Glue to page. • Insert key transparencies into Black slide mounts. Add to page with glue dots.

1. Cut slide mount in half. Ink with brayer.

2. Trace outline on foam board with stylus.

3. Cut out foam frame.

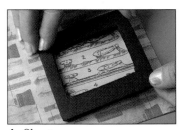

4. Glue to paper.

5. Fill with embellishments.

6. Add acetate to slide mount.

7. Glue slide mount to frame.

Using large slide mounts to make shaker boxes allows you to display 3D materials loosely in your scrapbook.

Jersey Shore

by Tim Holtz

MATERIALS: *Design Originals* Slide Mounts (#0975 Large, #0978 Black) • *Design Originals* Transparency Sheets (#0559 Alphabet) • *7 Gypsies* "Papier" paper • *Ranger* (mini brayer, Archival Cobalt ink pad) • *Crafter's Pick* (Memory Mount, The Ultimate!) • *Petersen Arne* vellum • Black foam board • Craft knife • Metal ruler • Cutting mat • Letters and game pieces • Mini brads • Shells • Clear acetate

INSTRUCTIONS: Brayer Cobalt ink to surface of frame. • Cut slide mount in half and place on Black foam core. Trace outline of slide with stylus tool. Cut using a craft knife and metal ruler (inside & out). • Glue slide mount to page. Fill with shells and glue to photos using Memory Mount • Cut acetate to fit frame and glue to top. • Glue slide mount to frame. • Glue shakers to page. • Embellish corners of shaker slides with mini brads. • Mat photo.
• Print text on vellum from computer. Attach to page with brads. • Insert alphabet transparency into small Black slide mounts Add to page. • Glue additional letters and game pieces to create title using The Ultimate!.

My first trip to the Jersey Shore with my friend Robin. We both had such a great time driving along the shore stopping to see Tillie at this Old landmark amusement park...

Here is a page to get those creative juices flowing! Follow the easy how-to photos on page 38 to see just how easy it is to give your pages a whole new 'dimension'.

Make a border with covered slide mounts framing charms.

Charms Border

by Jennifer Maughan

MATERIALS: *Design Originals* Legacy Collage Paper (#0538 Peter's Dream, #0553 Map) • *Design Originals* Slide Mounts (#0977 White) • *Bazzill* cardstock (Blue Linen, Navy Blue) • *EK Success* Charms • *Buttons Plus* hearts • *Jest Charming* dragonfly brads • Glue stick

INSTRUCTIONS: Glue Map to Navy Blue cardstock. • Cut slide mount in half at fold. Cover slide mount with Peter's Dream paper. Glue Blue Linen cardstock to slide mount. Mat with torn Navy Blue cardstock. Glue to border strip. Add charms.

Display your family photos in these sticker covered frames.

These heritage frames were made by covering slide mounts with nostalgic stickers. The mats add an extra nice touch.

Through the Years

by Jennifer Maughan

MATERIALS: *Design Originals* Legacy Paper (#0480 Green Floral, #0498 TeaDye Tapestry) • *Design Originals* Slide mounts (#0975 Large) • *Design Originals* Transparency Sheets (#0556 Word Tags) • *Design Originals* The Ephemera Book (#5207 p. 7) • *Bazzill* Linen cardstock (Blue, Black) • *Stickopotamus* (Nostalgique Floral Delight sticker, typewriter stickers) • *All Night Media* border punch
INSTRUCTIONS: Tear Green Floral. Glue to Blue Linen. • Glue transparency words on TeaDye Tapestry. Cut out in tag shape. Glue to page. • Cover slide mounts with Floral stickers. • Insert photo. • Punch Blue linen mat and layer on Black. Glue to page. • Add typewriter stickers.

Placing a niche on a page adds depth and interest. Slide mounts make great windows.

Life is a Journey

by Susan Keuter

MATERIALS: *Design Originals* Legacy Collage Paper (#0528 Watches) • *Design Originals* Slide mounts (#0978 Black) • *Design Originals* Transparency Sheets (#0556 Word Tags, #0561 Travel) • *Bazzill* cardstock (Maroon, Blue) • *Artistic Expressions* foam core • *Flea Market by Sharon Soneff* computer font • *Ink It!* key & lock charms • *Simply Charming* watch charm • *Making Memories* star brads • Craft knife
INSTRUCTIONS: Glue Watches paper to foam core board. • Cut hole the size of slide mount opening in foam core. Glue Blue cardstock into hole. Glue charm in place. • Cut slide mount in half at hinge. Tape transparency inside slide mount. Glue slide mount over hole. • Mat photos. Glue in place. Glue journaling box to page.

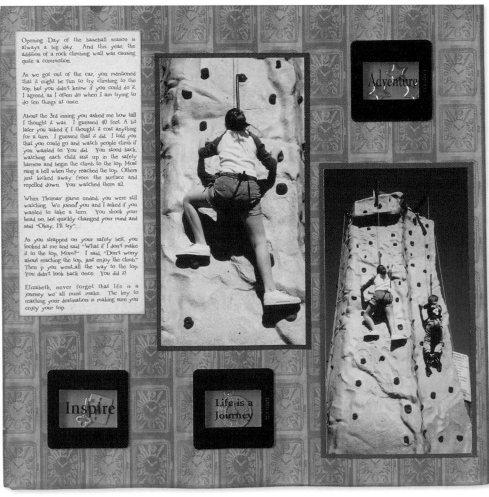

Elegant heritage pages give sparkle to black and white photos. Slide mounts can be covered and colored to match the page, or left alone to complement the photo. Even better, make two pages and use both techniques.

Whatever you choose, remember to have fun!

Mother

by Shirley Rufener

MATERIALS: *Design Originals* Legacy Collage Papers (#0485 Blue Stripe, #0486 Blue Floral, #0498 TeaDye Tapestry, #0549 Shorthand) • *Design Originals* Slide mounts (#0975 Large, #0977 White, #0978 Black) • *Design Originals* Transparency Sheets (#0556 Word Tags, #0559 Alphabet, #0562 Nature) • Cardstock (Black, Oatmeal, Black satin) • *Aleene's* Memory Glue • *StazOn* ink pads (Ultramarine, Olive Green, Pumpkin, Azure, Timber Brown) • 5 dauber applicators • Large stencil brush • *Fiskars* deckle edge scissors • 1/16" hole punch • Adhesive sizing • Metallic Gold leaf • Adhesive foam dots • Gold 22 gauge wire • 2 antique brass charms • *Xyron* Solutions Mounting Tape • Rubbing alcohol

INSTRUCTIONS: **Background**: Triple mat Black, Oatmeal, Stripe. • Deckle edge photo and mat on Black satin cardstock. Glue in place.
Title: Layer Shorthand paper and Alphabet Transparencies in Black slide mounts. Punch 1/16" holes in slide mounts and hook together with wire loops. Adhere to page with foam dots.
Transparencies: Color tint back with StazOn ink. Let dry. Apply thin layer of adhesive sizing to back. Let dry. Press metallic leaf over entire back surface. Burnish with finger. Fill in any holes with more leaf. • Punch 1/16" holes. Attach wire links and charms. • Secure slide mounts with foam dots. • **Large Slide Mount**: Apply Ultramarine ink onto large slide mount with dauber leaving White areas. Apply Olive and a touch of Pumpkin ink randomly. Immediately stipple with rubbing alcohol. Press and rotate brush in a spiral motion to remove some ink. • Age edges with Brown. Let dry. Secure "Mom" transparency behind window with Adhesive Runner. Glue Tapestry paper inside mount. Tape mount closed. • Secure to page with mounting tape.

Metal leaf makes transparencies glitter.

Bold black letters complement the black slide mounts on this page.

Apply rubbing alcohol to ink for an interesting watercolor effect.

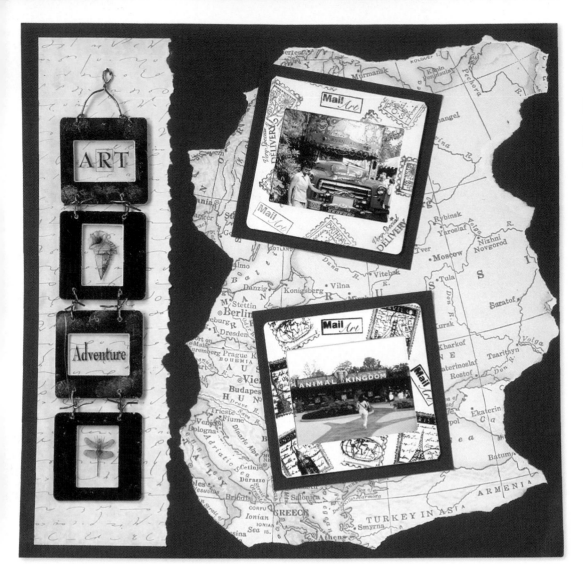

Twisted copper wires
make interesting
hangers. They create
a rougher texture than
jump rings.

Create unique slide mounts with
ink and rubber stamps.

Create a frame that matches the theme of your photo and scrapbook page by stamping slide mounts. Hanging a slide mount border gives you a place to display other memorabilia from your trip.

Art Adventures

by Pam Hammons

MATERIALS: *Design Originals* Legacy Collage Paper (#0549 Shorthand, #0553 Map) • *Design Originals* Slide mounts (#0975 Large, #0978 Black) • *Design Originals* Transparency Sheets (#0556 Word Tags, #0562 Nature) • Black cardstock • *Hero Arts* Travel Postage rubber stamp series • Black *StazOn* ink pad • 1/16" hole punch • 20 gauge Copper *Artistic Wire*

INSTRUCTIONS: Tear Map paper. Glue to Black cardstock. • Tear Shorthand paper. Glue to left side of page. • Stamp large slide mounts with travel stamps and StazOn. Let dry. • Insert photos in slide mounts. Mat with Black cardstock. Glue to page. • Tape transparency sheets inside Black slide mounts. Punch holes for wire. Wire slide mounts together. Make hanger on top mount. Glue to Shorthand paper.

1. Punch the holes.

2. Connect slide mounts together with wire.

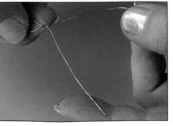

3. Make a wire hanger.

4. Attach the hanger to the top of the slide.

1. Wipe ink across the map paper using sponge.

2. Sponge edges of paper.

3. Roll edges of the paper to texture.

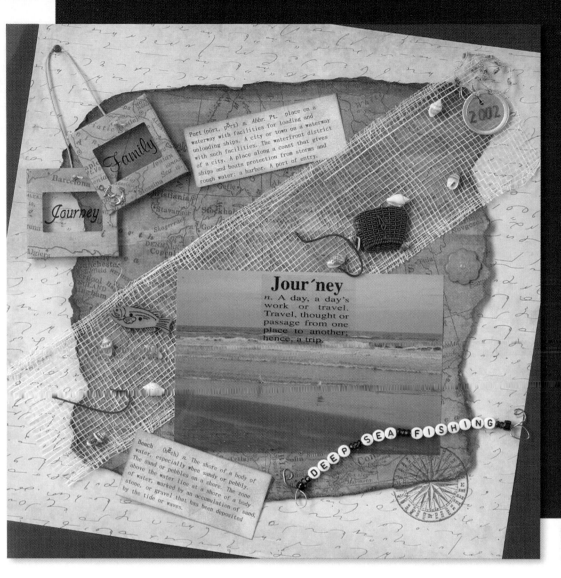

Sand colored papers and mesh texture generate the seaside feeling in this page. Charms and beads enhance the theme.

Family Journey

by Katrina Hogan

MATERIALS: *Design Originals* Legacy Collage Paper (#0549 Shorthand, #0553 Map, #0487 Rust Linen) • *Design Originals* Slide mounts (#0977 White) • *Design Originals* Transparency Sheets (#0556 Word Tags, #0558 Script) • *Making Memories* round vellum tag • *Jesse James* buttons • *Magic Scraps* (beads, shells, anchor charm) • Copper *Artistic Wire* • *Stop N Crop* mesh • *7 Gypsies* Walnut ink • Rubber Stamps (*Hero Arts* numbers; *Uptown Design* compass) • *ColorBox* Ink Pads • *Adornaments* Fibers • Fishing hooks • Small brass brad • Tan string
INSTRUCTIONS: **Age patterned paper**: Wipe diluted Walnut ink across Map paper with a sponge. Tear paper to shape, then sponge edges of paper with Walnut ink. Roll the edges of the paper to texture. • **Cover slide mount**: Apply spray adhesive to grid side of Map paper. Press slide mount down firmly. Use craft knife to cut around edges and inside of slide mount. Add transparency and seal two halves of slide mount together. Punch a hole in top center. Thread fiber. Attach string to page with brad. Add charm. **Assemble page**: Trim Shorthand paper and glue to Rust Linen background. Glue aged Map paper in place. Stamp with compass. Lay mesh diagonally and glue shells, buttons and hooks. Print "Port" and "Beach" definitions on cardstock. Sponge to age. Glue in place. Assemble covered slide mounts with transparencies. Glue together. Add anchor charm and string. Attach string to page with brad. Glue slide mounts in place. Adhere "Journey" transparency to photo. Glue photo to page. Curl wire end. String beads. Curl other end. Glue to page.

Use slide mounts to make your title.

Picturesque Provence

by Mary Kaye Seckler

MATERIALS: *Design Originals* Legacy Collage papers (#0553 Map) • *Design Originals* Slide Mounts (#0977 White) • *Foofala* (5" x 7" slide mounts, brass frame) • 12 photos • 2 pieces 5" x 7" book board • 2 pieces 7" x 9" Blue cover paper • *Fancifuls* (3 Brass brads, 2 Brass filigree charms, arrow charm) • *Red Line* tape • Rubber stamps: (*Hampton Art Stamps* fleur de lis; *Hero Arts*' Picturesque' alphabet; *Penny Black* filigree) • *Printworks* Yorktown Blue ink • Glass beads (6 Blue, 6 Green) • 3 yards Black waxed linen thread • 2 needles • PVA glue • Glue dots
INSTRUCTIONS: Make hole punching template using diagram. • See stitching instructions and diagrams. • Sew slide mounts together with Black waxed linen using star book stitch. • On every other slide mount, add 4 beads as you sew. • Tape photos into frames. Tape frames closed. • Add charms and titles to pages. • Tape ribbon to outside of first and last frames. Cover book boards with cover paper. Glue cover boards to first and last slide frames. • Trim Map paper to size. Edge with Blue ink. Glue to cover. • Stamp fleur de lis and 'picturesque' with Blue ink. Trim and tape to cover. • Add brass brads to brass frame. Slide Provence title into frame. • Stipple slide frame with Blue ink and stamp filigree. Mount with thick foam tape. Glue arrow charm to center of slide frame. Adhere to cover with glue dots. Tie ribbons to close book.

Post Cards from Home

by Mary Kaye Seckler

MATERIALS: *Design Originals* Heritage Paper (#0412 Travel Postcards) • *Design Originals* Slide Mounts (#0978 Black) • Black core mat board • 6 glass beads • *Making Memories* (metal letters, metal glue) • *Limited Edition* 'Home' game tiles • Green ribbon • 36" Black waxed linen thread • *Red Line* Tape • *Tyvek* shipping envelope • Gold pen • Acetate (optional)
INSTRUCTIONS: Reduce scrapbook paper by 35% on a color copier. • Cut out postcards with margin all around. Prepare slide mounts for stitching by gluing a piece of Tyvek in the fold for reinforcement. (Optional: Tape acetate to both windows of slide mounts . On first and last slide mounts, use only one piece of acetate.) Outer windows are covered by mat board. • Tape postcards behind windows. • Make a hole-punching template with 2" square cardstock: Fold in half. Mark four holes on fold as in diagram. Refold so that pencil marks are inside fold. Nest template in fold of slide mount. Punch holes. Repeat for all slide mounts. • Sew slide mounts together using Star Book stitch (see stitching diagrams), adding two glass beads to every other slide mount. • Tape slide mounts closed with Red Line Tape. Label slide mounts with Gold pen. • For covers, cut Black core mat board to size. Tape ribbon and covers to front and back slide mounts with Red Line Tape. • Tie book closed with ribbon. Add title on front with metal glue.

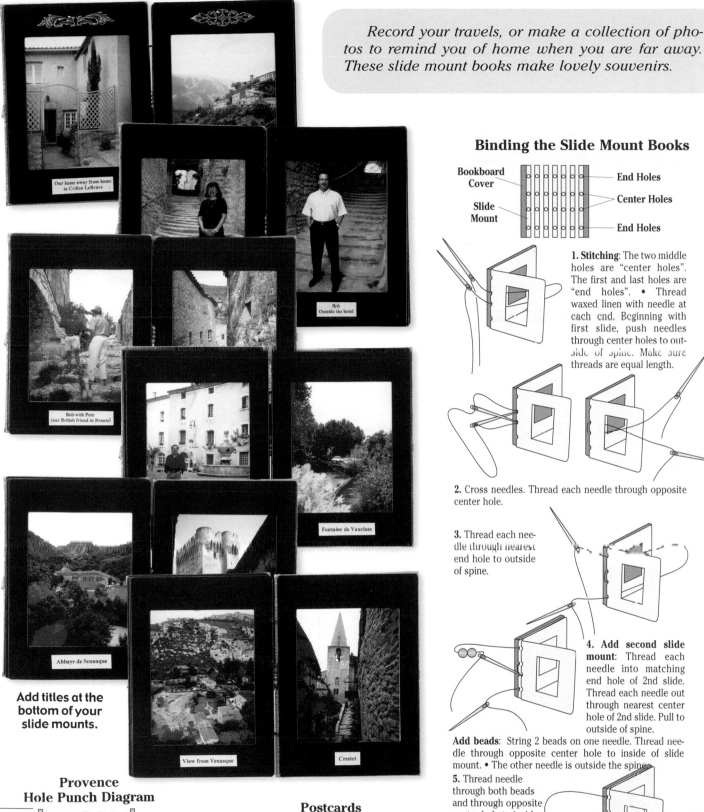

Record your travels, or make a collection of photos to remind you of home when you are far away. These slide mount books make lovely souvenirs.*

Add titles at the bottom of your slide mounts.

Binding the Slide Mount Books

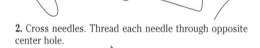

Bookboard Cover — End Holes
Slide Mount — Center Holes
— End Holes

1. Stitching: The two middle holes are "center holes". The first and last holes are "end holes". • Thread waxed linen with needle at each end. Beginning with first slide, push needles through center holes to outside of spine. Make sure threads are equal length.

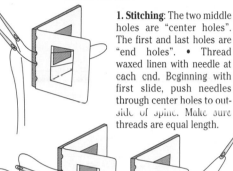

2. Cross needles. Thread each needle through opposite center hole.

3. Thread each needle through nearest end hole to outside of spine.

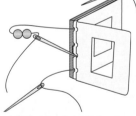

4. Add second slide mount: Thread each needle into matching end hole of 2nd slide. Thread each needle out through nearest center hole of 2nd slide. Pull to outside of spine.

Add beads: String 2 beads on one needle. Thread needle through opposite center hole to inside of slide mount. • The other needle is outside the spine.

5. Thread needle through both beads and through opposite center hole to inside of slide mount.

6. Thread each needle to outside of spine through nearest end hole.

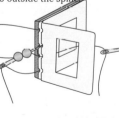

7. Add third slide mount: Repeat steps 2 through 5 until all slide mounts and back cover is added. Tie off with a square knot on the inside of the last slide.

Provence Hole Punch Diagram

$1^1/_2$"
$1^1/_2$"
1"
$1^1/_2$"
$1^1/_2$"

7"

Spine End View

Postcards Hole Punch Diagram

1/8"
1/2"
1/2"
1/2"
1/8"

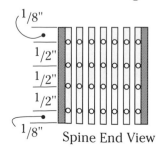

Spine End View

Scrapbooks - Slide Mounts 45*

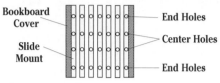

Butterfly Book

by Shari Carroll

MATERIALS: *Design Originals* Legacy Collage Papers (#0526 Two Ladies, #0527 Pink Diamonds, #0530 Mom's Sewing Box, #0542 Father's Farm, #0547 Dictionary) • *Design Originals* Slide Mount (#0977 White) • *Design Originals* Transparency Sheets (#0562 Nature) • *Mead* small composition book • Brown eyelets • *Hero Arts* rubber stamps • *Memories* Dye Ink • *American Accents* Rust Treatment • Black waxed string • Craft knife • Eyelet setter • *Red Line* tape
INSTRUCTIONS: Cover composition book with Legacy Collage Legacy papers. • Glue stamped flowers to cover. • Spray slide-mount with Rust treatment, continuing with recommended top coat. • Punch small holes in slide-mount. Set eyelets. Lace with Black string. • Cut measuring tape from Mom's Sewing Box paper. Glue to slide mount. • Trace opening of slide-mount onto front cover. Cut cover with craft knife. • Tape transparency inside slide-mount. Glue to cover over opening. • Cut inside sheets (15-20). Glue "Bingo" paper so it shows through the hole.

Transform a composition book with a niched collage cover, or make your own book using covered slide mounts sewn together with a simple shoe-lace style binding. Using velvet paper gives a classic feel to the cover of your book.

1. Cut a hole in the cover of the notebook.

2. Cut the niche inside to match the cover hole.

3. Tape the transparency inside the cover.

4. Place the decorated slide mount over the niche.

Time Flies Book

by Katrina Hogan

MATERIALS: *Design Originals* Legacy Collage Paper (#0550 TeaDye Script) • *Design Originals* Slide Mounts (#0975 Large, #0977 White) • *Two Busy Moms* vintage fibers • *Autumn Leaves* vellum • *Nunn Design* dragonfly charm • *Making Memories* (Time Flies word charm, nail-heads) • Velvet paper • Spray adhesive • Craft knife • Paper piercing tool
INSTRUCTIONS: **Front Cover**: Glue front side of slide mount to velvet paper. Trim and cut out center with craft knife. • Spray adhesive on back of Script paper. Adhere back of slide mount to paper. Trim, including center. • Place vellum between two halves of slide mount. Tape mount shut. • **Pages:** Cut two slide mounts at hinge. Cover 3 slide mounts with Script paper completely. • Cover remaining slide mount with Script paper for inside, velvet paper outside. • **Binding:** Punch holes in front cover. Line front cover up with second page. Mark holes placement. Punch holes. • **Threading:** Begin with bottom hole. Lace like a shoe. Knot fibers together.

This lovely memory album, made from one slide mount and a bit of cardstock, captures a moment in time. The textured cover is both beautiful and simple to make.

Memories

by Susan Keuter

MATERIALS: *Design Originals* Legacy Collage Paper (#0552 Travels) • *Design Originals* Slide Mount (#0975 Large) • *Design Originals* Transparency Sheet (#0558 Script, #0560 Objects) • *Bazzill* Linen cardstock • *Suze Weinberg* Ultra Thick Embossing Enamel • Gold ink pad • *Waxy Flax* fibers • *Ink It!* charms • Eyelet • Gold embossing powder • Embossing ink pad • Nonstick craft sheet • Heat gun

INSTRUCTIONS: Open slide mount. Lay flat. Cover with Gold ink. Let dry. Cover with embossing ink and UTEE. Heat until bumpy. • Tape transparency and paper inside slide mount. • Cut Linen paper 13 1/2" x 3 1/2". Fold paper in quarters. Glue top and bottom to slide mounts. • Print journaling and glue in place. • Mat photos with torn Travels paper and Green linen. Glue in place. Record dates. • Punch hole in corner and set eyelet. Tie charms to book with string.

This is the back of the "Memories" book. Create a place to sign your work.

These are the only pictures I have of Grandma as a child. I cherish them. I imagine what was going on at the time of the pictures. I know the baby picture was taken in Ohio by a door-to-door photographer. (Aunt Elsie was scolded for letting a stranger photograph the baby!) As a one year old, the portrait was professional. Her face I recognize in my children's. The snapshot is from a bridge in Pennsylvania. All total, small details. But details that will live in my stories and dreams.

one year old 1919

Imagine having a record of your great grandmother. Make this book and your great grandchildren won't have to just imagine.

1918

dream

1921

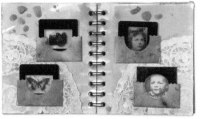

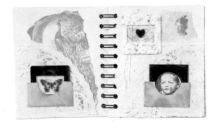

Time Flies

by Pam Hammons

MATERIALS: *Design Originals* Legacy Collage Papers (#0527 Pink Diamonds, #0528 Watches, #0538 Peter's Dreams, #0550 TeaDye Script, #0552 Travels, #0489 Rust Floral, #0501 TeaDye Clocks) • *Design Originals* Slide Mounts (#0975 Large, #0977 White, #0978 Black, #0979 Round) • *Design Originals* Transparency Sheets (#0556 Word Tags, #0560 Objects, #0561 Travel, #0562 Nature) • *Adornaments* fibers • Paper doily • Key charms • Gold foil • Rubber Stamps (*Inkadinkado* clock; *JudiKins* 2512H Woman's face; *Hero Arts; Hot Potatoes*) • *Memories* Black ink • Watch parts • Buttons • *DMD* 4" x 5" spiral notebook • *Cat's Eye* (chalk, ink) • *Delta* Paint Jewels • Diluted instant coffee • Craft knife • Metal ruler • *Gem-Tac* glue • Acetate • 2 #1 coin envelopes • Cutting mat

INSTRUCTIONS: **Coffee Staining**: Mix 1 Tbsp water at a time with 1/2 tsp instant coffee until mix looks like thin syrup. Use fingers or sponge to dab onto surface being stained. Let dry. • **Cover**: Coffee stain TeaDye Clocks. Glue to cover. • Use craft knife and metal ruler to cut niche 1/2" from bottom and sides • Fill niche with Gem-Tac glue and clock parts. • Cut large slide mount in half. Coffee stain slide mount. Tape transparency to slide mount. Glue to cover. • Binding decoration: Stain both side of small white slide mount. Insert transparency. Glue shut. Punch hole in corner. String fibers through hole in slide mount and through binding rings. Tie knot.

Greatest Gift

by Pam Hammons

MATERIALS: *Design Originals* Legacy Collage Papers (#0538 Peter's Dreams, #0550 TeaDye Script, #0552 Travels) • *Design Originals* Slide Mounts (#0975 Large, #0977 White, #0978 Black) • *Design Originals* Transparency Sheets (#0556 Word Tags, #0562 Nature) • *ColorBox* Ice Blue Fluid Chalk ink pad • *McGill* Circle punch • *Adornaments* fibers • Charms • Beads • Paper doily • *Hero Arts* rubber stamps • *Cat's Eye* ink • Craft knife • Metal ruler • *Gem-Tac* • Cutting mat

INSTRUCTIONS: Use craft knife and metal ruler to cut niche 1/2" from bottom and sides • Glue Travels paper to cover, including niche. • Fill niche with Gem-Tac glue and beads. • Cut large slide mount in half. Ink slide mount. Tape transparency to slide mount. Glue to cover. • Binding decoration: Enclose transparency in Black slide mount. Punch hole in center. String fibers through hole in slide mount, through binding rings. Tie knot.

• Glue 1st page of book to cover. Glue old text and cut outs from Watches paper to page. Coffee stain. Stamp with Black ink. • Glue cardstock to back of 2nd page. Glue torn TeaDye Clocks and Watches paper to page. Stamp. Stain page. Cut window. • Cut small White slide mount at hinge. Stain and stamp. Tape acetate to slide mount. Glue to page.

• Stain cardstock and slide mount half. Stamp page. Glue slide mount to page. • Stamp face on cardstock. Tear and glue in place. Stain and stamp page.

• Stain pages. Glue doily in place. • Sponge ink on 2 coin envelopes. Cut envelopes in half. Glue to page. • Insert transparency into 3 Black slide mounts. Place in envelope. • Use round slide mount to mark circle. Cut hole in page. Place round slide mount in pocket.

• Glue TeaDye Script to page. Attach key charms. Cut slide mounts in half. Stain and stamp slide mounts. Add transparencies. Glue in place.

> *Designing your own altered style artwork is fun with slide mounts and niches. You'll need a spiral notebook to start.*

• Sponge ink on pages. Tear Peter's Dreams paper. Glue in place. Stamp page and round slide mount. Glue slide mount to page. • Butterfly transparency from previous page shows through window of slide mount.

• Ink pages. Cut scraps in curves. • Foil back of elephant transparency. Glue scraps, transparency, and foil to page. • Place mat behind page. Cut horizontal curves across page. Cut scrap paper in curves. Weave papers. • Add foil. Stain round slide mount. Tape transparency to back. Glue to page.

• Ink and stamp pages. Drizzle Paint Jewels onto slide mount. Spread with fingers. • Apply Diamond Glaze to back of transparency. Drip Blue, Purple and Green ink from bottle. Smear with spoon. Back with crumpled tissue paper. Let dry. Tape to slide mount. Glue to page.

• Glue 1st page to cover. Sponge ink. • Tear Travels paper. Glue to page. Glue doily to page. • Sponge ink and cut coin envelope in half. Glue to page. • Insert transparency into Black slide mount. Put slide mount in envelope. • Use cutting mat behind page 1. • Make window to page 3 by cutting circle to fit slide mount hole through doily and page. You should see child's face in window. Glue envelopes in place. Put round slide mount in envelope. • Stain White slide mount. Tape transparency to back of slide mount. Glue to page.

Bon Jour

by Pam Hammons

MATERIALS: *Design Originals* Legacy Collage Paper (#0526 Two Ladies) • *Design Originals* Slide Mounts (#0977 White) • *Design Originals* Transparency Sheet (#0558 Script, #0561 Travel) • Cardstock (Brown, Peach) • *Jacquard* Super Copper lumiere paint • Amber Clay *ColorBox* Fluid Chalk • *Hero Arts* Italian Poetry stamp • Gold jump ring
INSTRUCTIONS: Glue Peach and Two Ladies paper to Brown cardstock. • Apply Amber Clay chalk to slide mounts. Paint with Super Copper. Stamp with Black ink. • Tape transparency to slide mount. Close mount. • Punch hole in corner. Add Gold jump ring.

Liberty Border

by Jennifer Maughan

MATERIALS: *Design Originals* Legacy Paper (#0499 TeaDye Music) • *Design Originals* Slide Mounts (#0977 White) • Cardstock (Navy Blue, Red) • *Karen Foster* stickers • *Nostalgique* stickers • *Jest Charming* Star Brads • *Inkadinkado* (Illuminata stamp, Black ink) • *Card Connection* (vellum envelopes, cards) • Double-stick tape
INSTRUCTIONS: Glue TeaDye Music paper to Blue cardstock. • Tear Red cardstock and stamp all over. Glue to border. • Cut slide mount in half at fold. Cover slide mount with stickers. Attach to border with double-stick tape. Add star brad. • Tape the envelopes with the cards in place.

Life is a Journey

by Jennifer Maughan

MATERIALS: *Design Originals* Legacy Collage Paper (#0548 Passport) • *Design Originals* Slide Mounts (#0977 White) • *Design Originals* Transparency Sheet (#0561 Travel) • *Nostalgique* stickers • Coins • Charms • Rust cardstock • Foam tape
INSTRUCTIONS: Glue Passport paper to Rust cardstock. • Cut slide mount in half at fold. Cover slide mount with stickers. • Use foam tape to create slide mount shaker box. • Tape transparency to top slide mount. Tape Rust cardstock to back of bottom slide mount. Place coin or charm inside. Place top slide mount over tape.

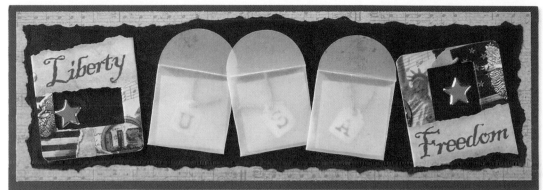

Face Border   *by Jennifer Maughan*

MATERIALS: *Design Originals* Legacy Collage Paper (#0530 Mom's Sewing Box, #0537 Faces of Friends) • *Design Originals* Slide Mounts (#0977 White) • *Bazzill* Black Linen cardstock • *EK Success* Charms • *Button Ups* buttons • Brown thread • Glue stick
INSTRUCTIONS: Glue pieces of Mom's Sewing Box paper to Black Linen cardstock. • Cut slide mount in half at fold. Cover slide mount with Mom's Sewing Box paper. Glue cut outs from Faces of Friends paper to slide mount. Glue to border strip. Add charms. • Thread buttons. Glue in place.

Wild West   *by Pam Hammons*

MATERIALS: *Design Originals* Legacy Collage Paper (#0412 Travel Postcards, #0493 Brown Linen, #0547 Dictionary) • *Design Originals* Slide Mounts (#0979 Round) • 2 Cow charms
INSTRUCTIONS: **Coffee Staining**: Mix 1 Tbsp water at a time with 1/2 tsp instant coffee until mix looks like thin syrup. Use fingers or sponge to dab onto surface being stained. Let dry. Glue elements on border strip.

Time Flies

by Katrina Hogan

MATERIALS: *Design Originals* Legacy Collage Papers (#0527 Pink Diamonds, #0535 Ruth's Letter) • *Design Originals* Slide Mount (#0979 Round) • *Design Originals* Transparency Sheets (#0560 Objects) • Tan Cardstock • *Milton Bradley* game tiles • *Making Memories* metal verses • 7 *Gypsies* clock charms • *EK Success* (playing card, typewriter keys, vellum tags, fibers) • Jute • *Mead* composition book • Rubber stamps (*JudiKins* crackle rubber stamp; *Limited Edition* clock) • Spray adhesive • Craft knife • Tissue paper (Black, Red) • Clock parts • Mesh • Silver embossing powder • Embossing ink pad

INSTRUCTIONS: **Cover**: Spray back of Pink Diamonds paper with spray adhesive. Glue to cover. Trim excess paper using a craft knife. Cover binding with tissue paper. • Stamp crackle pattern onto Tan cardstock with light Brown ink. Sand the paper to age. Tear and crumple paper. Wet and roll edges. Glue to cover. • Layer torn Ruth's Letter paper, mesh, tags, and charms onto cover. • Punch hole near top of cover. Thread jute through hole and around cover. Add key charm. Tie a bow. • **Slide mount**: Emboss slide mount with Silver several times. While still warm, stamp clock in corners. Insert transparency. Punch hole in slide mount. Add fibers. Glue to cover.

Stamp embossing while it is still warm for added texture.

Cover slide mount with collage paper and add charms for variety on your page.

Attach fibers and charms to match the image. Collage the background.

Aspire Journal

by Shari Carroll

MATERIALS: *Design Originals* Legacy Collage Papers (#0527 Pink Diamonds, #0528 Watches, #0530 Mom's Sewing Box, #0542 Father's Farm, #0549 Shorthand, #0550 TeaDye Script, #0551 Legacy Words, #0552 Travels) • *Design Originals* Slide Mount (#0977 White) • *Design Originals* Transparency Sheets (#0561 Travels) • *Mead* composition book • Brown brads • *Hero Arts* rubber stamps • *Memories* Dye Ink • Black waxed string • *Red Line* tape • *Two Peas In A Bucket* bookplate • *Sower* letter stickers • *Making Memories* letter tags • Foam tape

INSTRUCTIONS: Collage book cover and slide mount using Legacy Papers, leaving the Black spine cloth uncovered. • Tape transparency inside slide-mount. • Punch small holes in slide mount and tie on small tags using Black waxed thread. • Foam tape slide-mount to cover. • Stamp flowers in desired areas. • Trim "aspire" from Words papers and place in bookplate. Attach with brads. • Glue stickers in place and attach fibers.

Keys to Happiness

by Amy Hubbard

MATERIALS: *Design Originals* Legacy Collage Paper (#0551 Legacy Words) • *Design Originals* Slide Mount (#0975 Large) • *Design Originals* Transparency Sheet (#0560 Objects) • Burgundy mulberry paper • *Pearl Ex* (Super Russet, Antique Gold) • *Adornaments* fiber • Key charms • *Rebecca Sower* Typewriter Key stickers • Ultra Thick Embossing Enamel • Spiral notebook • Brown eyelets • Stamps • *Versamark* ink pad • Glue stick • 1/8" hole punch

INSTRUCTIONS: Remove wire from steno notebook. Remove cover. • Trim Legacy Words paper to size of cover. • Stamp randomly with nature stamps in versamark ink. Brush stamped images with Super Russet and Antique Gold Pearl Ex. Crumple paper. Glue crumpled paper and mulberry paper to front of notebook cover. Let dry. • Cover slide mount with Brown dye ink. Let dry. • Cover slide mount with versamark ink and add three layers of UTEE, adding Super Russet Pearl Ex to each layer. Ink texture stamp with Gold dye. Press into warm embossed slide mount. Set aside. • Follow original holes to punch 1/8" holes through the paper. Tear mulberry paper. Glue to cover. Add typewriter stickers. • Insert transparency in slide mount. Add eyelets across bottom. Tie key charms with fibers through eyelets. • Place notebook cover back on notebook and wind the wire back through. Glue slide mount to cover.